Delegation Skills for Leaders

An Action Plan for Success as a Manager

Third Edition

Lloyd Finch and Robert B. Maddux

A Crisp Fifty-Minute™ Series Book

1-800-442-7477 • 25 Thomson Place, Boston, MA • www.courseilt.com

Delegation Skills for Leaders

An Action Plan for Success as a Manager

Third Edition

Lloyd Finch and Robert B. Maddux

CREDITS:

Product Manager:	**Debbie Woodbury**
Editor:	**Marguerite Langlois**
Production Editor:	**Genevieve McDermott**
Production Artists:	**Nicole Phillips, Rich Lehl, and Betty Hopkins**
Manufacturing:	**Denise Powers**

For more information contact:

Course Technology
25 Thomson Place
Boston, MA 02210

Or find us on the Web at **www.courseilt.com**

For permission to use material from this text or product, submit a request online at: www.thomsonrights.com

Any additional questions about permissions can be submitted by e-mail to: thomsonrights@thomson.com

Trademarks

Disclaimer

ISBN 1-4188-6263-0
Library of Congress Catalog Card Number 2005933075
Printed in the United States of America
1 2 3 4 5 PM 08 07 06 05

Learning Objectives for

DELEGATION SKILLS FOR LEADERS

The learning objectives for *Delegation Skills for Leaders* are listed below. They have been developed to guide the user to the core issues covered in this book.

The objectives of this book are to help the user:

1) Understand the role of delegating as part of the management process
2) Identify delegation strengths and remove the obstacles that may get in the way of successful delegation
3) Determine the appropriate tasks to delegate and select the right people to do them
4) Learn the important management skills required to successfully delegate
5) Acquire an understanding of how delegation can help employees develop, grow, and become even more responsible

Assessing Progress

Course Technology has developed a Crisp Series **assessment** that covers the fundamental information presented in this book. A 25-item, multiple-choice and true/false questionnaire allows the reader to evaluate his or her comprehension of the subject matter.

To download the assessment and answer key, go to www.courseilt.com and search on the book title or call 1-800-442-7477.

Assessments should not be used in any employee-selection process.

About the Authors

The original version of this book, *Delegating for Results*, was written by Robert Maddux, who worked extensively with organizations and people in transition. The late Mr. Maddux designed and conducted management skills seminars in Canada and Europe, consulted on training films, and authored several best-selling management books.

Lloyd Finch, another best-selling Crisp author, has added his expertise to this third edition, retitled *Delegation Skills for Leaders.*

Lloyd Finch is a consultant, trainer, and writer who has worked with a variety of corporate clients. His firm, Alpha Consulting Group, specializes in assisting clients with training in the areas of customer service improvement and general management skills. He has written and produced training videos and won coveted national awards for three of them. He is experienced and successful as a seminar leader, speaker, and training designer.

He has written several top-selling books, including *Telephone Courtesy and Customer Service*, *Success as a CSR*, *Twenty Ways to Improve Customer Service*, and *Call Center Success*.

Before starting Alpha Consulting Group, Lloyd was in corporate sales and sales management.

Lloyd can be reached at alphaconsulting@prodigy.net.

Preface

One of the most difficult tasks of leadership is to effectively delegate assignments to others. Delegating is a skill that must be put into practice very carefully. When successfully done, more is accomplished, which reflects favorably on the manager, the team member, and the work unit. The new title of this book, *Delegation Skills for Leaders*, addresses the subject of delegation as an essential tool for leaders.

Leaders want to be successful, and to be competitive they will work hard to achieve their goals. Delegation is a process that is designed to help the leader in the quest for success. But there are also risks. Unsuccessful delegated assignments reflect poorly on the manager. This book offers suggestions, ideas, and a step-by-step approach that will reduce these risks and guarantee delegation success.

Managers must focus on planning, organizing, motivating, and controlling. They also need to develop employees who can improve their job performance and become more valuable to the organization. In this way organizations grow and their accomplishments soar. A key method of ensuring stronger employee performance is to delegate responsibility to the individual. Most employees want increased responsibility and are usually willing to take on tough assignments. Strong leaders understand this and strive to develop others by delegating meaningful work assignments.

Delegation is not some mysterious art available only to a chosen few. It is a basic management skill that involves a process that can be learned. By putting into practice the techniques, ideas, suggestions, and skills presented in this book, you will become more effective at delegating. This will enhance your abilities as a leader, allowing you to achieve even more success.

Good luck!

Lloyd C. Finch

Table of Contents

PART 1

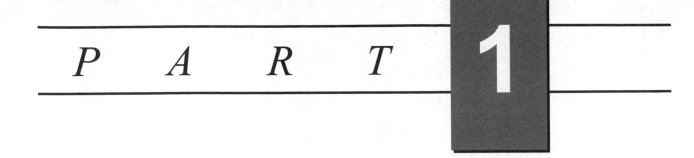

The Role of the Manager

Management and the Delegation Process

Management is the process of working through individuals and groups to accomplish organizational goals and objectives. To accomplish this, leaders need to recognize the difference between management skills and operational tasks and increase their knowledge of delegation.

A manager is responsible for executing the management process. How well this is done will determine the success of the manager and the work unit. The management process requires skills—skills that are innate in a few leaders but are learned by most of us.

Management practitioners and scholars vary widely in their definitions of the management process. These differences are usually nothing more than a choice of words. Some consolidate similar functions into broad categories; others prefer an extensive listing of individual functions.

The Four Functions of Management

For the purposes of this book, the management process consists of four primary functions: planning, organizing, motivating, and controlling. Good delegation, the subject of this book, requires skill in all four.

The next few pages will give you an opportunity to review your understanding of these functions.

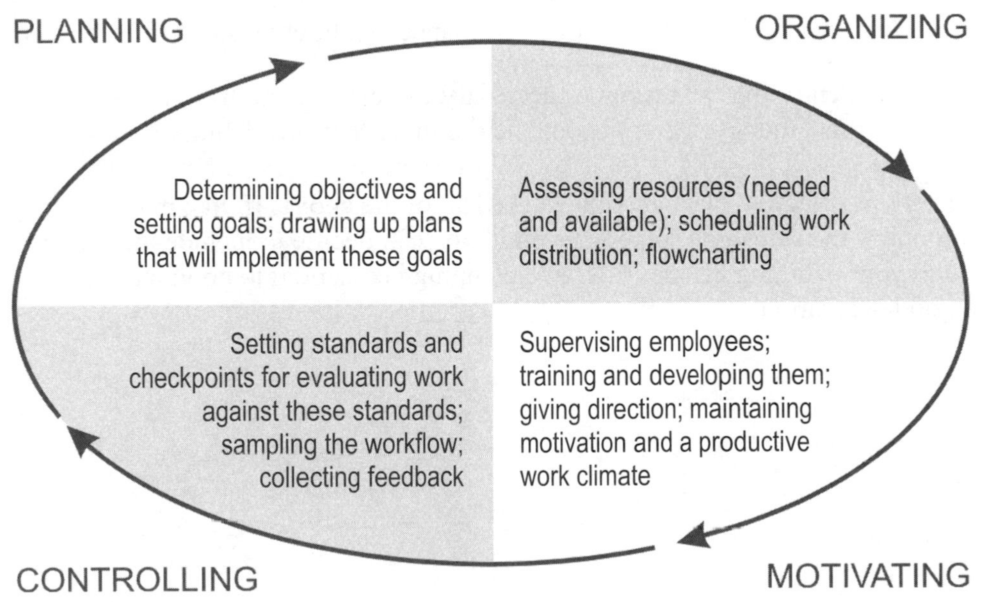
PLANNING
ORGANIZING
Determining objectives and setting goals; drawing up plans that will implement these goals
Assessing resources (needed and available); scheduling work distribution; flowcharting
Setting standards and checkpoints for evaluating work against these standards; sampling the workflow; collecting feedback
Supervising employees; training and developing them; giving direction; maintaining motivation and a productive work climate
CONTROLLING
MOTIVATING

Planning

Planning is the thinking that precedes doing. It means setting goals and objectives for an organization, and preparing plans and schedules to accomplish those goals. Strong managers plan well and effectively communicate that planning to their employees. Everyone within the work unit needs to know what the plan is and how it will affect them.

To see if you are an effective planner, review the following list of the elements of planning. Check (√) those statements that describe the tasks you always or almost always use in planning.

❑ 1. Interpreting goals and objectives passed down from above as the result of planning performed at a higher level

❑ 2. Considering the thoughts and ideas of the employees who are directly involved, as well as your thoughts and ideas

❑ 3. Formulating and establishing policies and procedures to accomplish goals and objectives; making certain new policies don't interfere with performance

❑ 4. Examining alternatives and selecting the activities that will lead to the desirable results

❑ 5. Establishing timetables and completion targets in keeping with priorities

❑ 6. Determining standards of performance and how results will be measured

❑ 7. Identifying the resources necessary for task accomplishment—people, time, money, material—and determining their availability

If you are an effective planner, you checked all of the above. If, like many of us, you found some steps you sometimes omit, you can decide to include these more often in your planning efforts. Effective planning is essential to good management and good delegation.

Delegating Planning Steps

Although we have not discussed the how-to aspects of delegating as yet, let's consider delegating some of the planning process to direct reports. For now, we will do it in a general way.

It is important in any organization to get employees to buy into the plan. One way to do this effectively is to get them involved in developing the plan in the first place. Employees will be more enthusiastic and accepting of a plan they helped create than one that is just delivered in a top-down fashion. This can be accomplished through delegation.

Having decided to have team members participate in the planning process, let's think about what can be delegated to them. Because you have overall responsibility for the planning, it is very unlikely that you are going to delegate all the responsibility. But there are activities that can be delegated that will help you complete the planning process.

Of the seven planning elements listed earlier, which ones do you think your employees could be involved in? Write the numbers of those planning elements here:

____

Depending on your creativity, you might list any or all of the seven planning elements. But the most likely ones are #2, #3, #4, and #6.

Let's work through an example using element #3:

Formulating and establishing policies and procedures to accomplish goals and objectives. Making certain that new policies don't interfere with subordinate performance.

Policies and procedures tend to help or hinder performance, so they have a direct effect on your team. Since you are an enlightened manager, you would like to have employee input as to what policies and procedures will help their work process. Let's examine a case study of what might be delegated.

CASE STUDY: Involving Employees in Planning

Marcy has twelve direct reports. Her two strongest performers are Stuart and Kim and she is interested in developing their skill level and abilities. Marcy is working on a plan that will result in overall expense reduction of 10% for her work unit over the next 12 months.

She knows the objective will be difficult to achieve without the full support of her people. Marcy has decided that her team could complete planning element #3. She would like to involve all of her people in the process. Marcy will retain final approval of any policies or procedures that are developed.

Answer the following questions in the space provided below. Some tips and suggestions are provided in parentheses. What do you think would work best for you?

1. Suppose you were in Marcy's position. How would you describe the overall task you want your employees to complete? (Tip: Planning element #3)

   ___

   ___

   ___

2. Whom would you involve, just Kim and Stuart or the whole group? (Tip: The more the better)

   ___

   ___

   ___

3. How would you structure it? (Tip: Two groups or one? a leader for each group?)

   ___

   ___

   ___

4. How will you receive feedback from the group? (Tip: Leader reports back, a written report, meet with the entire group, or other method?)

   ___

   ___

   ___

CONTINUED

CONTINUED

5. During this delegation process, what will you, as the manager, be doing? (Tips: Monitor everything that goes on, attend team meetings, discuss progress with the leaders you have chosen, keep a hands-off approach, or other activity)

____

____

____

____

Congratulations! You have just successfully delegated a work assignment.

Compare your answers with the author's suggested responses in the Appendix.

Organizing

Once planning is underway, organizing becomes essential. Resources—people, capital, equipment, raw materials, and facilities (all elements of the planning)—must be brought together in the most productive way to accomplish objectives.

In the list below, check (√) the elements that you think organizing should provide:

- ❑ 1. Appropriate staffing—the right number of people with the essential skills to perform the work that has to be done
- ❑ 2. Delineation of responsibility and authority
- ❑ 3. Alignment of major functions and structuring of the component parts into effective work units and teams
- ❑ 4. Documentation such as an organizational chart, to depict how responsibility has been assigned and authority delegated
- ❑ 5. Development of a communications model or system for reporting and coordinating tasks between people and organizations
- ❑ 6. Facilities and equipment needed for task accomplishment
- ❑ 7. A clear and concise statement concerning goals and objectives

If you checked all seven boxes, give yourself 100%!

Look over this list of the seven organizing tasks and ask yourself where you might delegate some of your organizational activity. As in the planning phase, there are multiple opportunities in the organizational phase to delegate. While much depends on the work environment and the skill of your employees, their involvement could result in a stronger organizational plan.

Note here some or your current organizational tasks you might consider delegating:

____

____

____

____

____

____

____

Motivating

Motivation, along with planning and organizing, plays an important part in the level of performance achieved in any endeavor. Effective delegation can be a powerful motivating factor.

To check your views on motivation, review the following statements and indicate which are true and which are false.

True False

____ ____ 1. The needs and desires of employees have little bearing on motivation.

____ ____ 2. It is important to create an environment in which employees can meet their needs while meeting the needs of the organization.

____ ____ 3. Results generally improve when people are able to participate in deciding what the results should be.

____ ____ 4. Motivation to achieve results improves when employees are recognized for their contributions.

____ ____ 5. Studies have shown that communication has very little to do with motivation.

____ ____ 6. Coaching and training tend to raise personal levels of motivation.

____ ____ 7. Motivation to achieve results usually increases as employees are given authority to make decisions affecting those results.

____ ____ 8. Good managers pay close attention to the way employees respond when they assign work.

Compare your answers with the author's suggested responses in the Appendix.

For more information, read *Motivating at Work*, by Twyla Dell, a Crisp Series book by Thomson Learning.

Controlling

Controlling is concerned with results. It involves follow-up to compare results with plans and to make adjustments when results differ from expectations. There is probably more confusion among managers about controlling than any other aspect of managing.

The confusion for many managers about controlling centers on the amount of control to apply. Far too often, leaders have too many controls and as a result they over-manage. The reason for this over-management is that managers want to meet their objectives so they attempt to control and manipulate the results. But employees who are trained and responsible normally produce the best results and they perform their jobs with few controls. Every employee's skill level is different and therefore the amount of control placed on his or her work performance should differ. Managers need to recognize this fact and strive for a reasonable balance. Every manager has employees who are self-sufficient and few controls need to be placed on them. Others may need a rigorous set of controls in order to get their job done.

Managers may also get confused as to how to produce the best results. Managers cannot control the results of their work units. But they can control the key work activities that lead to results. Note that we are talking about key work activities and not every work activity. Controls over these key activities are set up for the work unit and all employees understand they must be successfully completed because the unit's results are dependent upon it. Responsible and skilled employees successfully complete these key activities as a matter of course and as a result they need little control or supervision. When all or most of the work unit performs in this manner, the manager's controls are truly work unit-oriented rather than individually-oriented.

The final potential for confusion regarding control is the simple fear of giving up too much control. Being the leader means being in control. Or at least that's what most managers have been told. As we take on a new management job, too many of us set about establishing ourselves as someone who is in absolute control of the work unit. Often there is immediate conflict between the manager and the employees who are responsible and used to running their own jobs. The manager tries to exert more control than may be necessary and the employee balks. Often the manager is acting out of fear—fear of not being perceived as a manager who is in control of things. This situation can be avoided if the manager will just realize that she has the authority, power, and command to run the work unit because she is the manager and every employee knows this. The unreasonable fear that drives some managers to strive for absolute control is something every manager needs to guard against.

One way to approach the control issue is to take into consideration these three principles:

1. Work unit and individual employee controls must be reasonable and established not out of fear but for the benefit and success of the work unit.
2. Identify as few key control activities as possible.
3. Focus on the needs of the employees and the work unit and less on the needs of the manager.

In the following list of statements about controlling, identify those you believe to be true and those you believe to be false.

Controlling requires:

True	False	
____	____	1. Devising methods to accurately assess whether goals, objectives, or standards have been met in a timely and cost-effective manner
____	____	2. Punishing employees who have missed their targets
____	____	3. Formulating methods to measure and evaluate various resources for future planning purposes
____	____	4. Developing and maintaining a feedback system so that the manager will know the current status of the key activities—this feedback system may be formal or informal in design
____	____	5. Limiting employee authority to minor details
____	____	6. Reporting the status of activities and projects to those who need to know

Compare your answers with the author's suggested responses in the Appendix.

CASE STUDY: The Sales Funnel

As a leader, if you want to achieve consistent and desirable results, monitor the activities and provide enough control to ensure the best results of delegated activities.

Jon is a sales manager. He has learned that his salespeople can make at least two sales a week if they will make 10 customer presentations per week. Two sales a week per salesperson exceeds Jon's sales objective. To make a sales presentation, the salespeople must first secure an appointment with the customer. To get 10 appointments they have to make 30 telephone calls.

Suppose you had Jon's job. What activities of the salespeople would you try to control? How might you do it? Write your answers below.

____

____

____

Compare your answers with the author's suggested responses in the Appendix.

Getting Work Done in Organizations

Management is a leadership effort to integrate and effectively use a variety of resources to accomplish an objective. It applies to all organizations, whether they are businesses, hospitals, non-profits or government entities. Managers will do well to remember there is no one best way to plan, organize, motivate, or control. As a leader, you must continually increase your knowledge of the management concepts and draw upon them until you find a winning combination.

One factor is central, however, to every management task. That factor is *delegation*. You must know what is expected of your unit, when it is expected, and how best to employ human resources to obtain the desired results. This means assigning work in a planned and thoughtful way. And all team members must know what is expected of them and when it is expected.

Delegation is giving people things to do. Management is accomplishing organizational goals by working through individuals and groups. It is easy to see that the two are closely entwined. And it is obvious that the manager who is not delegating is not achieving the best possible results.

The manager is responsible for all the work of the unit and to get it all done must delegate carefully and successfully. Not every manager is up to the task. Consider the case study that follows.

CASE STUDY: The Do-It-Yourself Manager

Joanne was a capable and enthusiastic professional. She was promoted to manage a group of nine people doing work very similar to her own past assignment.

She began her new position with a great deal of knowledge about her team's jobs and responsibilities. She felt less comfortable about her new responsibilities as their manager. Joanne knew that she had greater expertise than her team members and could do the work better and faster than they could. She decided to focus on getting the work out and initiate further job training and delegation at a future date.

Joanne did not pass on any major assignments to her employees; she did much of the work herself. As time passed, her hours of work increased steadily and she was less and less available to her employees—and to her own manager, with whom coordination was important. Her employees were given routine work, received no training, and actually knew very little about major projects in progress.

Finally, after 60 days, Joanne's manager called her in to discuss her performance. Joanne looked forward to the meeting because she felt that she was working very hard and doing a good job. Is Joanne in for a surprise?

What would you say to Joanne if you were her manager? Write your thoughts and suggestions below:

____

____

____

____

____

____

____

Compare your answers with the author's suggested responses in the Appendix.

CASE STUDY: The Hands-Off Supervisor

In this case study, the supervisor is Sean and he is responsible for 10 direct reports. He acts very differently from Joanne.

Sean prided himself on his organizational skills and his ability to get results. As the result of a reorganization, three of his top performers were replaced with new hires. Sean assigned the new people the same work the previous employees had been doing. He explained to them that he was delegating the responsibility and the authority to do their delegated assignments. He further said, "I don't want to interfere with how you run your job. It's the results that I'm interested in."

He went on to state that he is a hands-off manager and doesn't like to be bothered with the details. Finally he said, "Run your own jobs and if you need help let me know. If I don't hear from you, I'll assume everything is okay." The new employees got to work, as did the rest of the work unit. Sean went back to his usual routine of not doing very much. He spent much of his time working on his next promotion.

The Result: Less than 60 days went by and Sean was in trouble. His results had fallen off and two of his new employees had made major mistakes in their work. The mistakes were costly to Sean's group and to other groups who were depending on the information Sean's unit supplied for them.

Sean's manager, Roberto, was extremely upset and demanded an explanation. Sean blamed the new subordinates for the mistakes. He told Roberto, "They just aren't as sharp as the old crew." Roberto replied, "Did you work closely with them and monitor their performance?" Sean didn't have a good answer. Roberto continued, "What have you been doing down there?" Sean still didn't have much of an answer.

The Solution: Sean clearly needs to change his management style. His former employees were strong and were able to carry him, but they are gone.

If you were Sean, what specific changes would you start with to improve the situation?

____

Compare your answers with the author's suggested responses in the Appendix.

Joanne and Sean: These case studies represent two extremes of delegation. Joanne did everything herself, and Sean delegated everything. Successful leaders find a balance and learn when, where, and to whom they can delegate.

Technical, Human, and Conceptual Skills

Many supervisors and managers approach their jobs much like Joanne and Sean and fall into a similar trap. They do not seem to have a thorough understanding of how to delegate effectively. Part of their problem is not considering the differences between technical, human, and conceptual skills and how these skills apply to their position. Think of them this way:

Definitions		
Technical Skills	**Human Skills**	**Conceptual Skills**
Ability to use knowledge, methods, and equipment to perform specific tasks, learned through experience and training	Ability and judgment in working with people, including an understanding of motivation and leadership	Ability to understand the complexities of the overall organization and where one's own unit fits into the total picture

First-level supervisors need considerable technical skill because they are often required to train and develop new employees and technicians. Senior managers, however, do not always need to know how to perform all the specific tasks at the operational level. They need to understand how the functions are interrelated. The common denominator that is crucial at all levels is human skill.

As you move up in management, you must learn to delegate jobs requiring technical skill to your employees. This gives you time to learn the human and conceptual skills increasingly required of you.

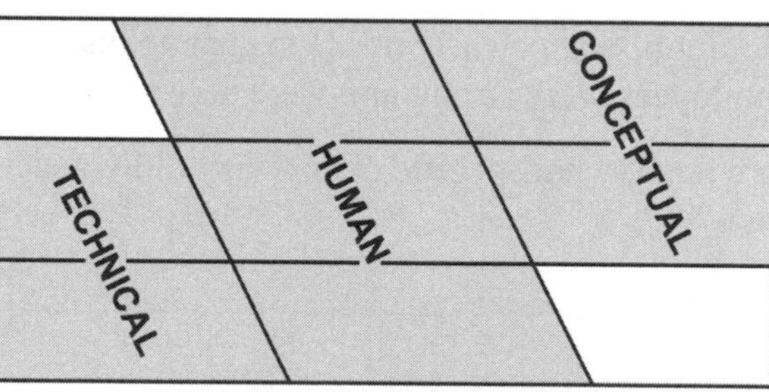

What Can Delegating Do for Me?

New managers like Joanne often assign a low priority to delegation because they are unsure of how to go about it and do not see the benefits. Sometimes leaders fail to delegate because they are fearful about giving up the responsibility and authority needed to do the task or job. Some actually think delegation is more trouble than it is worth.

Managers like Sean, on the other hand, are willing to let go of all responsibility and authority. Sean seems nearly fearless and does not consider the overall consequences of his approach. There is a place for delegation in every work unit. The advantages of delegating far outweigh the disadvantages.

Some advantages of good delegation are listed below. Check (√) those you think are most important for you to achieve in your current situation.

- ❑ More work is accomplished and deadlines can be met more easily
- ❑ Employees become involved and committed
- ❑ The assignment of specific responsibility and authority makes control less difficult
- ❑ Employees grow and develop
- ❑ Human resources are used more fully and productivity improves
- ❑ Individual performance can be measured more accurately
- ❑ Compensation, including merit increases, can be more directly related to individual performance
- ❑ A diversity of products, operations, and people can be managed effectively
- ❑ Distant operations can be managed with less travel and stress
- ❑ Employee satisfaction and recognition are enhanced
- ❑ The manager has time for planning, organizing, motivating, and controlling
- ❑ The manager is freed to do those tasks only managers can do

Add any other advantages you can think of, especially those that apply directly to your situation, in the spaces below.

- ❑ ______________________________
- ❑ ______________________________
- ❑ ______________________________

P A R T **2**

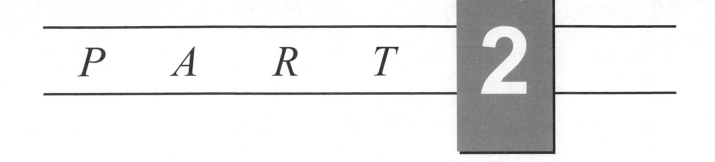

Analyzing Personal Delegation Skills

How Well Do I Delegate?

Self-assessment is an ongoing management skill. Strong leaders continually assess their skills; this allows them to continue to develop and become even stronger performers. You can do the same thing.

The self-assessment exercises in this section will provide you with considerable insight into your willingness and ability to delegate. These exercises can also help you identify areas of concern regarding how you currently delegate.

Identify Your Strengths

This exercise is an opportunity to identify your strengths and determine where improvement would be beneficial. Read each statement and circle the number that best describes you. The higher the number, the more the statement describes you. When you have finished, total the numbers circled in the space provided.

1.	Each of my employees knows what I expect of them.	7 6 5 4 3 2 1
2.	I involve employees in goal setting, problem solving, and other important issues confronting my work unit.	7 6 5 4 3 2 1
3.	I place my personal emphasis on planning, organizing, motivating, and controlling, rather than completing tasks others could do.	7 6 5 4 3 2 1
4.	When assigning work, I select the assignee thoughtfully.	7 6 5 4 3 2 1
5.	When problems occur on projects I have delegated, I give the employees a reasonable chance to work them out for themselves.	7 6 5 4 3 2 1
6.	When I delegate work to team members, I make certain they understand what to do and what is expected.	7 6 5 4 3 2 1
7.	I see delegation as one way to help employees develop their skills, and I assign work accordingly.	7 6 5 4 3 2 1
8.	I support and help employees in emergencies, but I do not permit them to leave work for me to do.	7 6 5 4 3 2 1
9.	When I assign work, I stress the results desired but also show my willingness to help the employee where needed.	7 6 5 4 3 2 1

10. When I delegate a project that affects others, I make sure everyone concerned knows who is in charge. 7 6 5 4 3 2 1

11. When delegating work, I grant the authority to do the job based on an employee's experience level. 7 6 5 4 3 2 1

12. I hold my employees responsible for results of delegated tasks and projects. 7 6 5 4 3 2 1

Total: __________

A score between 72 and 84 suggests you are on target. A score between 48 and 71 indicates you are getting by, but could improve. Anything below 48 means you need to make changes.

Am I Employing the Right People?

If you are to have a strong team to whom you can delegate, you need to hire team members with that thought in mind. Human resources are the most critical part of any manager's success. Good people help ensure profitability, productivity, growth, and long-term survival. If the people you select on your team are successful, you will be successful.

Selecting the Right People

Listed below are some critical elements in employee selection and placement. Indicate how well you perform by checking the appropriate box.

	Do Well	Should Improve
1. I analyze job requirements thoroughly before beginning the selection process.	❑	❑
2. I always probe for objective evidence of a candidate's skills, knowledge, past successes and failures, dependability; and attitude toward work, co-workers, supervisors, and customers.	❑	❑
3. I determine the type of project and task responsibility the applicant has had in previous positions, and how he or she has handled authority.	❑	❑
4. I make sure each applicant understands the job requirements and expected standards of performance.	❑	❑
5. I describe my idea of teamwork to applicants and ask them to assess how they would work under team conditions.	❑	❑
6. In making a selection decision, I evaluate facts carefully and avoid coming to premature conclusions or stereotyping.	❑	❑
7. People I hire are placed in positions where there is potential for success.	❑	❑

Developing Employees to Handle Complex Tasks

Some of us do not have the opportunity to personally hire all the people who work for us. Often new managers inherit an existing group. That means taking on the strong performers as well as those who may need improvement.

Regardless of the situation, every employee deserves an opportunity to learn how to handle complex tasks and assignments. Delegation is the perfect tool for this opportunity. How well you use delegation as a way to develop your employees may well be the key to your success.

Your Skill at Delegating to Develop People

Answer the following, using the letter that best describes your behavior.

A = Always

F = Frequently

O = Occasionally

N = Never

_____ I use delegation to build new employee skills and strengthen existing ones.

_____ I prepare people properly for assignments I delegate to them.

_____ I review performance against expectations with each employee, and we jointly identify training that will strengthen results.

_____ I listen to employees' growth objectives and support them through delegation when I can.

_____ I make certain the employees have everything they need to successfully complete the delegated assignment.

_____ I make myself available for employee questions and discussion.

_____ I monitor the delegated assignment without interfering.

_____ I provide an evaluation of the delegated work for the employee.

_____ I avoid playing favorites with my team members in making assignments.

_____ I ask my employees what they think of my delegation process.

If your employees participate in formal training, answer these additional questions.

______ I talk in advance to employees selected for training, to emphasize the importance of the training to their job and their delegated assignments.

______ When employees are in training, I have their work covered so that they can concentrate on what is being taught.

______ I help employees develop an action plan to apply their training to the job and to any additional assignments I delegate.

______ I ask the employees for an evaluation of the training program and whether it would be suitable for other members of the team.

______ I delegate work to employees that allows them to apply the new techniques and skills learned during training.

Ideally all of your answers will be marked *A* for *always*. Most managers will have at least a few statements marked something other than *always*. These are the areas that you can focus on during your next delegation.

Symptoms of Poor Delegation

Let's continue with self-assessment by examining the symptoms of poor delegation. Identifying such symptoms will help you select activities that further develop your delegation skills.

There are many symptoms of poor delegation. They are readily seen in the work unit, in the work habits of the manager, the attitude of the employees, and the productivity of the group. Check (√) the symptoms that are visible in your work unit.

- ❑ We frequently miss deadlines.
- ❑ I am reluctant to delegate.
- ❑ I am far too busy to spend much time talking with my team members.
- ❑ Employees do not feel that they are empowered to do their jobs.
- ❑ No one in the unit is ever ready for promotion.
- ❑ I often overrule my employees' decisions.
- ❑ Sometimes it is unclear who is in charge of a project.
- ❑ My team members are often reluctant to make decisions.
- ❑ As plans change, my employees are not always informed in a timely manner.
- ❑ Employees have been assigned tasks they were not ready for and could not handle without constant supervision.
- ❑ I sometimes intervene in a project or assignment without informing the delegatee.
- ❑ Employees have requested transfers to other units.
- ❑ The communications flow between my direct reports and me is sporadic, incomplete, and often not timely.
- ❑ I feel that I am just putting out one fire after another in trying to clean up after my employees.
- ❑ My more talented team members seem bored and frustrated much of the time.
- ❑ I try to control too many details of my employees' work.

If you checked more than one or two of the above statements, you should look carefully at your delegation practices and ask yourself why these conditions exist. Note here the symptoms that you feel are priorities for you to change as you improve your delegation skills:

____

____

____

Common Barriers to Delegation

Ineffective delegators often rationalize their inadequacies. They may face or create obstacles (real or self-imposed) that hold them back from becoming more effective.

In the following list of statements, indicate those that affect your delegation practices by checking (√) *yes*. If they do not affect you, check *no*. For accurate results, think about each statement carefully and be totally honest.

Yes	No	SELF-IMPOSED OBSTACLES
___	___	I prefer to perform operating tasks, not management functions, because I understand those tasks better and know how to do them.
___	___	I do not have time to train my direct reports.
___	___	I do not know how to delegate.
		Often I do not know when to delegate.
		I do not completely trust my employees, even my strong performers.
___	___	My employees will not like me if I expect too much of them.
___	___	Often I am not certain to whom I should delegate.
___	___	It is easier and quicker to do things myself.
___	___	We just cannot afford to make any mistakes.
		I am fearful about delegating too much.
		I am concerned about losing control.
		I am not very interested in the development of any of my current employees.

Yes	No	EMPLOYEE-IMPOSED OBSTACLES
___	___	I cannot delegate because my employees lack experience and competence.
___	___	My employees cannot adequately handle what they have.
___	___	My team members resist responsibility.
___	___	My employees fear my criticism and therefore avoid risk.
		My employees are not smart enough for me to safely delegate anything to them.

Yes	No	SITUATION-IMPOSED OBSTACLES
____	____	My manager expects me to handle the really important tasks personally.
____	____	My employees cannot be trusted to work on their own.
		The success of my work unit is totally my responsibility.
____	____	I have no one to whom I can safely delegate.
____	____	Most of my decisions are made under crisis conditions.

If you checked *no* to every statement, congratulations. That is a perfect score. Most likely, however, you have a few statements marked *yes*, indicating obstacles that affect your ability to delegate.

Keep in mind that as the leader you have the authority to make the changes needed. Note here the obstacles that you see as priorities to work on as you further develop your delegation skills:

____

____

____

____

____

____

____

To see how easily leaders allow these obstacles to interfere with their work performance, consider the following case study.

CASE STUDY: Letting False Obstacles Get in the Way

Jerry finished his first year as a supervisor with a great deal of satisfaction. He felt he had done a good job and had successfully delegated five key projects. When delegating, Jerry stayed very much involved and monitored nearly every detail of the project. He maintained timelines for each project to make certain they came in on time. Jerry looked forward to his year-end performance evaluation from his manager, Crawford.

Jerry was not pleased when Crawford described how disappointed she was in his performance. Jerry could hardly believe what he was hearing. Crawford said she saw three primary problems. First was Jerry's inability to properly delegate; second, his failure to develop his people; and third, his focus on personally completing tasks instead of managing.

Their conversation went like this:

Jerry: I don't understand. I delegated most of the key projects.

Crawford: You should have delegated all of them. Besides, you never really turned loose those you did delegate.

Jerry: I had to keep timelines to make certain.

Crawford: Your people should have control of those timelines. Who made the decisions on the projects?

Jerry: I did. I didn't have a choice. My people are too inexperienced.

Crawford: How are we ever going to develop them if you decide everything?

Jerry: Well, it's going to take time, I suppose. But right now I cannot trust them to take on a project and just run with it.

Crawford: You need to let them try. You can stay involved and monitor their work, but let them do it.

Jerry: I just felt we couldn't afford to make any mistakes.

Crawford: That's right. But you know how to manage these projects backwards and forward. Why haven't you trained your people?

Jerry: Well, I'd like to, but there just…

Crawford: Please don't tell me you haven't had time.

Jerry: Well, I haven't.

Crawford: And why is that?

CONTINUED

CONTINUED

Jerry: I'm just too busy.

Crawford: Busy working on projects when you should be managing your work unit.

Clearly, Jerry has some serious problems. Here are a few questions for you to answer about his situation.

1. Which four obstacles did Jerry offer as excuses?

   (1) ______________________________

   (2) ______________________________

   (3) ______________________________

   (4) ______________________________

2. How would you describe Jerry? Check (√) all that apply.

_______ A task-oriented supervisor who is not practicing management skills

_______ A supervisor who is about where he started in developing subordinates

_______ A supervisor who hasn't made much progress with delegating

_______ A supervisor who works hard but isn't managing his work unit

_______ Someone who doesn't understand delegating

_______ A supervisor who is holding his subordinates back

_______ A supervisor who needs to get out of his task-oriented comfort zone and start managing

Compare your answers with the author's suggested responses in the Appendix.

Removing Obstacles to Delegation

Jerry's situation is not uncommon. It is easy to allow these obstacles to get in the way. Let's briefly look at some ideas on how to remove them.

- **Self-Imposed Obstacles**

  The self-imposed obstacles are the easiest to deal with. You can often eliminate them by changing your attitudes. Perhaps you need to look at your team members in a more positive light. Place emphasis on what they can do rather than on what they cannot do. Become willing to give them a chance to get involved and to develop.

- **Employee-Imposed Obstacles**

  If you checked *yes* to obstacles in the employee-imposed obstacle category, you still have considerable control to make positive changes. Again, a more positive attitude toward your employees will be a big first step. If your team members do not have much experience, set up a plan to train and develop them.

  Let your goal be to turn those inexperienced employees into experienced ones. Every employee deserves a chance to develop and gain experience. Delegating tasks and projects, with your involvement, will help them develop. Do you have a developmental plan for each one of your employees? If not, it is time to get started—it will be a win-win situation for everyone.

- **Situation-Imposed Obstacles**

  Attitude also plays an important role with situation-imposed obstacles. Keep in mind that you are the leader and leaders take charge. The situation-imposed obstacles are under your control as much as anything else. Step up to the challenge and begin the process of eliminating them. If needed, develop a written action plan.

  Keep it simple by listing the positive steps you are willing to take to eliminate these obstacles. Maybe another manager or your own manager can help. Do not be afraid to ask. Find the most successful leaders in your organization and ask how they manage these challenges. Remember, strong leaders are willing to act and make changes; they never give up. You can do the same thing.

For Another View

For even more insight into how well you delegate, ask your employees what they think. Ask them to complete the exercises you just completed, only with you as the subject. They merely have to insert your name into most of the statements. Once they complete this delegated task, your insight about how you handle delegation will be even clearer. You will probably learn more about your management style as well.

Far too many leaders decide for themselves that they are doing a great job and seldom ask others for input. Strong leaders search for ways to improve their performance. All of us have room to improve and can do so if we are willing to assess ourselves and have an eagerness for self-improvement.

Leaders who rely only on their own assessment can easily have false perceptions. Let others, especially your direct reports, get involved in helping you improve. When you do, you will probably be complimented. That too will help you become an even stronger leader.

Dispelling Leadership Fears and Fallacies

A characteristic of good leadership is the ability to focus on facts and avoid half-truths, fantasies, drama, and other pitfalls. To start, consider the following statement. Do you think it's true or false?

There are no bad work units, only bad leaders.

The solution to a "bad" work unit can often be found in good delegating by an effective leader. And one of the keys to effective delegating is not getting stuck in the fallacies, fears, and myths that plague some leaders.

➢ **The Fallacy of Omnipotence**

This is the "I can do it better myself" syndrome. Even if it is true, the choice is not between the quality of the manager's work and the employee's work on a given task. The choice is between the benefits of your performance on a single task and the benefits of your spending time in planning, organizing, motivating, controlling, and developing an effective team.

Often supervisors act more like a subordinate than a leader of the work unit. They focus on tasks and avoid developing as managers by failing to get immersed in planning, organizing, motivating, and controlling. They do this because they are comfortable that way.

If you are skilled in the tasks of your work unit and less adept at management skills, it is easy to just keep on doing those tasks. That is your comfort level. But to grow and become a stronger leader you must stretch your comfort level. If you find yourself in this predicament, force yourself out of the task-oriented comfort zone and little by little start taking on management skills.

➢ **Fear of Being Disliked**

As a leader, would you rather be liked or respected? How about being both liked *and* respected? We all want to be liked, but we cannot let that desire be the motivation behind our management of the work unit. Leaders make tough decisions and often have to enforce unpopular policies. These management decisions cannot be made on the basis of whether you are going to be popular and well-liked.

It is okay to delegate a lot of work to your employees. It is okay to be critical. It is okay to decide who gets a raise and who does not. It is okay to say no. And it is okay to be a strong, stern manager who delegates and acts in a fair and consistent manner. Think of the managers you have liked and respected. Weren't they strong leaders? Employees rate leaders who make full use of delegation as good to excellent. Poor delegators receive lower ratings.

- **Lack of Confidence in Employees**

Managers who lack confidence in their employees should look to themselves for the answer. They are, or should be, in control of the situation.

If employees cannot handle delegated assignments, the manager either has incompetent people, has failed to provide them with appropriate training, has not worked closely enough with them, or has not made the effort to find out the extent of their capabilities. The remedy: Identify your employees' strengths and weaknesses, and train or replace those who still cannot meet standards.

- **The Fallacy that Employees Expect the Answers from Managers**

This fallacy allows managers to rationalize taking problem solving and decision making away from employees. It occurs when an employee takes a problem to a manager who says, "Why don't you leave it with me and I'll get back to you." The manager gets back to the employee with the solution. Often the employee wanted only to talk about the problem—and did not want the manager to solve it. Besides, when an employee leaves a problem on your desk, that is delegating upward, isn't it? Smart employee, don't you think?

- **The Myth that It Is Easier to Do It Than Explain It**

A manager who uses this excuse to justify doing an operating task that team members could learn is making a serious mistake. If you do not take the time to teach someone else the task, you will still be performing it far into the future. This consumes valuable time and effort that could be better spent on planning, organizing, motivating, and controlling.

Sometimes a manager truly cannot delegate. But as the chart below demonstrates, upward progression requires more and more delegating and less doing of operational tasks.

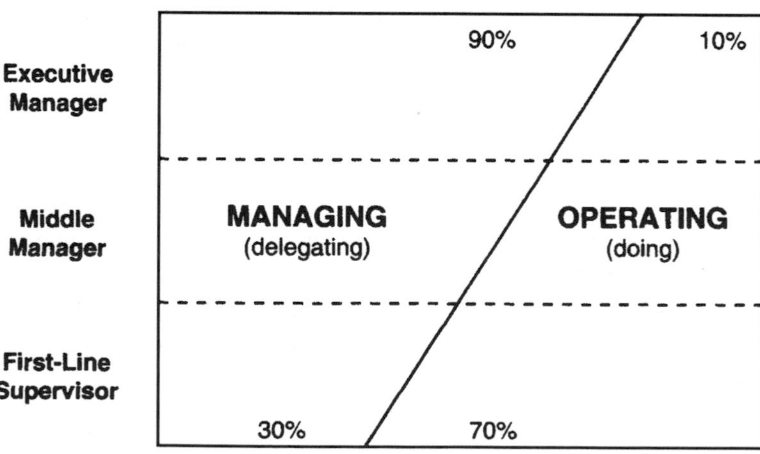

- **Fear of Losing Control**

  Most managers, especially new ones, have experienced some anxiety over losing control. Things can get very busy and chaotic. At times it may seem as if everything is out of control.

  At moments like this, it is important to set priorities and objectives that will lead you back to a feeling of control. A sure way to avoid this out-of-control situation is to place emphasis on the management process instead of on performing operational tasks that others could do.

Delegating Is a Choice

If you have done very little delegating, it is natural to hesitate to begin. But you have a choice to make:

- You can take the position that delegating is a valuable management tool that will help you improve as a leader and at the same time help your employees become stronger performers.
- You can take the view that no leader wants to give up authority and control by delegating an important assignment to an employee. If you are ultimately responsible for the completed assignment, why take the risk of delegating it?

Which choice represents your thinking at this point?

____

____

____

In this part, you have assessed your delegation skills in a number of ways. Review your work and note the delegation skills and approaches that you most want to improve as you learn more about delegation:

____

____

____

____

____

____

____

____

P A R T **3**

Preparing to Delegate

Analyzing Your Job

You are a manager, not an individual contributor. It is your job to employ your team members effectively to accomplish work unit goals. You must sort out the important from the unimportant and establish priorities. The more you delegate, the more employees can be expected to develop and successfully contribute to unit and organizational objectives.

To become an effective delegator, you must have your own job well in hand. This means periodically:

- Reviewing your duties and responsibilities as a leader. How have they changed? What new things do you have to learn? How do they affect your unit? What are the new challenges? What old practices need to be stopped?
- Reaffirming the primary objectives of your unit. Have there been any changes that affect priorities or that you need to communicate to employees?
- Highlighting the key results areas. What are the make-or-break factors in your assignment? What are the areas in which specific results are essential?
- Reexamining your workload to identify those few tasks only you can do.

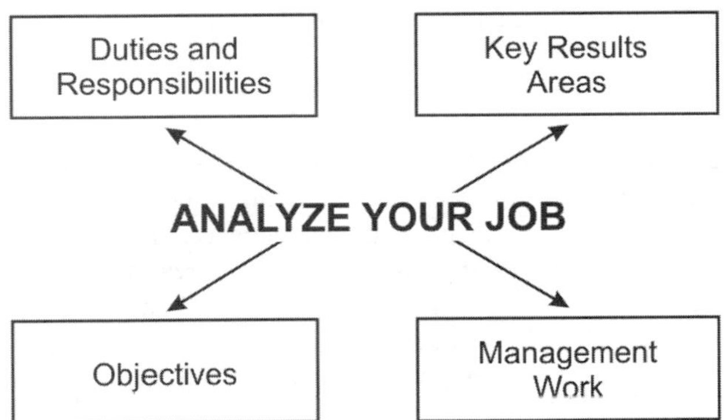

Let go of tasks and responsibilities that rightfully belong to your employees. That includes problem solving and decision making within their areas of responsibility. Be sure they are properly trained and help them as needed, but by all means give them a chance to do the job for which they were hired.

Deciding What to Delegate

Anytime you perform a task someone else could do, you keep yourself from a task *only you* can do. Managers usually delegate to give themselves more time to do complex and difficult management tasks, to improve productivity, or to develop their employees. Types of work you should consider delegating are listed in the exercise below.

Identifying Types of Work

Read the work described in the left column and then the description in the right column. List two possibilities from this type of work that you might delegate.

Decisions you make most frequently	Minor decisions and repetitive routines often consume a major portion of the day. You can delegate most, if not all, of these by teaching employees the policies and procedures that apply. They probably already know the details better than you.

List two possibilities:

1. ______________________________
2. ______________________________

Functions that are in your technical or functional specialty	These are usually operating tasks rather than management functions. You can teach others to do them. Your challenge as a manager is to motivate others to produce better results than you ever did as an individual performer. You can use part of the time you save to learn about other functions you supervise, so that you can manage them better.

List two possibilities:

1. ______________________________
2. ______________________________

Tasks and projects for which you are least qualified	Almost certainly, some of your employees are better qualified and can do parts of the job better than you. Let them.

List two possibilities:

1. ______________________________
2. ______________________________

Functions you dislike

Performing functions we dislike is distasteful, and we often put them off or do them poorly. Examine the likes and dislikes of your staff as well as their talents. You will nearly always find someone who likes the job and can do it well. If that employee needs training, provide it.

List two possibilities:

1. ____
2. ____

Work that will provide experience for employees

This makes growth in the present job a reality and helps keep employees challenged and motivated.

List two possibilities:

1. ____
2. ____

Assignments that will add variety to routine work

A change of pace is usually welcome and is often a good motivator for an a employee whose job is growing dull.

List two possibilities:

1. ____
2. ____

Activities that will make a position more complete

As employees become more proficient, they often have time to spare. Add complementary dutics and responsibilities to give their positions more substance.

List two possibilities:

1. ____
2. ____

Tasks that will increase the number of people who can perform critical assignments	Maximize the strength of the group by giving people the experience needed to back up one another during emergencies or periods of unusually heavy work.

List two possibilities:

1. ______________________________
2. ______________________________

Opportunities to use and reinforce creative talents	Employees are not creative in a stifling environment. Stimulate them with difficult problems and projects, and reward creative solutions.

List two possibilities:

1. ______________________________
2. ______________________________

Assignments that will provide direct exposure to related functions in other departments	Employees who perform related functions often learn from each other and come up with better ways to do the work.

List two possibilities:

1. ______________________________
2. ______________________________

Tasks that will bring high-potential individuals in contact with more senior management	This is a positive way for upper-level managers to develop an appreciation for the quality staff you are developing within the organization.

List two possibilities:

1. ______________________________
2. ______________________________

Now that you have completed this exercise, you have a list of work activities that might be delegated. Put this list into practice as you proceed to get more involved in delegating to your employees.

Targeting Areas of Delegation

The following illustration summarizes what you have learned so far and may help you identify areas where you can delegate more. As the illustration shows, there are four general work categories that fit with your delegation plans. When delegating, think of these four and make certain the work activities you delegate fit within these categories.

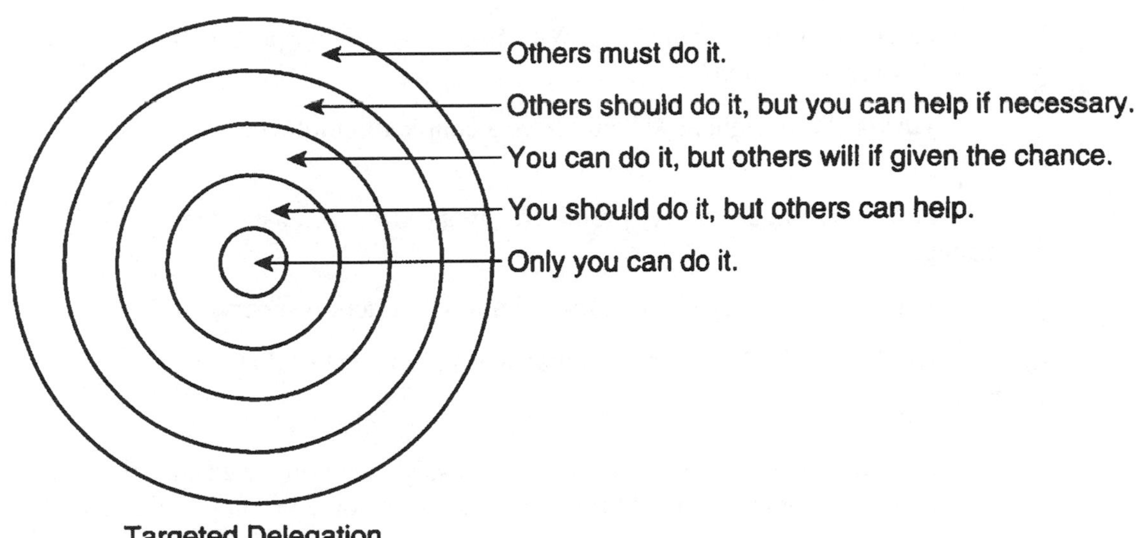
Others must do it.
Others should do it, but you can help if necessary.
You can do it, but others will if given the chance.
You should do it, but others can help.
Only you can do it.

Targeted Delegation

CASE STUDY: Sometimes Consistent Results Are Not Enough

Cynthia is well respected within her organization. Her responsibility as manager includes supervising a work unit of 14 team members. Cynthia is noted throughout the organization as a no-nonsense manager who is capable and gets things done. Cynthia's new manager, Crawford, congratulates Cynthia for her consistent results but also finds fault with her performance. The conversation goes like this:

Crawford: Tell me something. Why aren't any of your people on the "ready now" list for promotion?

Cynthia: Well, right now I only have a couple of employees who might qualify.

Crawford: Have you ever promoted anyone since you have been a manager?

Cynthia: Yes. Susan Gooden moved up to production supervisor.

Crawford: Didn't the previous manager set up most of that?

Cynthia: He did, but we worked closely to get Susan promoted.

Crawford: Your results are so strong I'm surprised you haven't been able to develop more of your people. Surely you must have some bright people down there?

Cynthia: Well, there's Jenny and Eames. I think they both have potential.

Crawford: Do you have a developmental plan for each of them?

Cynthia: No. I need to do that.

Crawford: What work activities, out of their normal routine, have you delegated to them? Any special projects or particularly interesting work assignments?

Cynthia: Well, everyone is so busy just trying to get their jobs done I haven't been able to do that.

Crawford: Let me ask another question. How much of your time do you spend training your employees, especially Jenny and Eames?

Cynthia: Again, I'm awfully busy to take much time out to train.

Crawford: But it's an important part of your job. Unless you delegate and train and try to develop your people, you're not being fair to them.

CONTINUED

CONTINUED

Cynthia took offense at Crawford's comment.

Cynthia: Not fair? I think I am a fair manager. I would say I am very fair.

Crawford: How can you be fair if you don't develop your people? You don't have a plan. As far as I can tell, you don't delegate anything. Only one promotion has come out of your group. Other people are being promoted or are being given better assignments over your people. I don't think you're being fair to your people at all. In fact, I think the people in your unit are sort of stuck in their places.

Cynthia clearly has problems choosing what to delegate. What types of work has she failed to delegate? (You may wish to review the types of tasks to delegate listed in the previous pages.)

____

____

____

____

Consider the choices you have made so far in the types of work you delegate to your employees.

1. Are you a fair leader? ____ *Yes* ____ *No*
2. If you answered *yes*, briefly explain why you are a fair leader.

   ____

   ____

   ____

   ____

3. If you answered *no*, briefly explain what you are going to do about the situation.

   ____

   ____

   ____

   ____

CONTINUED

CONTINUED

4. Suppose you are in a situation like Cynthia's. What major work activities from *your* job would you immediately delegate to Jenny and Eames? Keep in mind that you don't want a meeting like the one between Cynthia and Crawford. Assume that Jenny and Eames are capable of handling nearly any assignment. Use some of the possibilities you listed for delegation from the previous exercise.

   I will delegate the following to Jenny:

   ____

   ____

   ____

   ____

   I will delegate the following to Eames:

   ____

   ____

   ____

   ____

5. If you were Cynthia, what would be the first thing you would do? (Briefly describe what you would do other than delegate work activities to Jenny and Eames):

   ____

   ____

   ____

   ____

Compare your answers with the author's suggested responses in the Appendix.

Planning the Delegation

Deciding what to delegate is only the first step in the delegation process. Delegation, like most other management tasks, is most successful when it is planned. It may take a few minutes for simple tasks, or a few hours when the project is complex.

The Planning Checklist

Your planning should include at least the following considerations. In the checklist below, check (√) *Yes* if you already include the item in your planning; check *No* if you do not.

Yes	No	
____	____	1. What is the objective to accomplish?
____	____	2. What are the critical completion dates?
____	____	3. What standards will have to be met?
____	____	4. What decisions will have to be made?
____	____	5. How much authority can I delegate?
____	____	6. How much authority will I delegate?
____	____	7. What instructions or orders will the delegatee(s) be authorized to issue?
____	____	8. Does a budget need to be developed or followed?
____	____	9. Who will the delegatee(s) need to work with in my unit? In other units?
____	____	10. What information do I need to give?
____	____	11. How much do I want to be involved?
____	____	12. What feedback do I want and when do I want it?
____	____	13. Who will need to be kept informed of progress?
____	____	14. Do I need to tell others who is in charge?
____	____	15. To whom should I delegate?

If you checked *No* for any of the above items, plan on changing your delegation behavior so that you can include these items in your future planning. This checklist and the planning worksheets that follow will help you more effectively plan your next delegation.

TASK/PROJECT

Key Results Areas	Results Expected	Critical Timelines

ANALYSIS PLANNING SHEET

Standards to Be Met	Budget	Critical Interfaces	Frequency of Feedback

CASE STUDY: The Delegation Disaster

When Gino took over the systems group in the electronics division, he made up his mind to change the environment and the attitudes of the employees. His predecessor had not been an effective delegator or communicator. The employees had light workloads in a unit where the manger was totally swamped.

Gino immediately began to delegate assignments, including some decision-making tasks, that his predecessor had performed herself. He was surprised at the results.

His employees seemed to think he was pushing his work on them. Most of them complained they were neither trained nor paid to do the delegated assignments. It was not unusual for them to bring problems arising from their normal assignments to Gino for solutions, and they did not understand him saying, "Don't bring me problems, bring me solutions."

What has Gino overlooked in his approach to turning this situation around? Make your comments in the space below.

____

____

____

____

____

____

____

____

____

____

____

____

____

____

Compare your answers with the author's suggested responses in the Appendix.

Selecting the Right Person

The planning phase, prior to assigning work, is the manager's opportunity to organize and schedule the distribution of work. The quality of your preparations will largely determine the success of the delegation. Managers who fail to include delegation in their planning are usually those who keep far too much work to themselves and focus on operational tasks rather than on the management process.

After you complete your plan and analysis of what to delegate, you need to identify the appropriate person to perform the selected work assignment. Some of the many things to consider are included in the list below. Keep in mind that you really do not know what people can do until you give them a chance under the proper conditions.

Selection Factors

Answer the following questions in your selection process. The result will be better delegating decisions:

- How does the delegated work match up with the employee's abilities?
- Will the employee respond favorably to increased responsibility?
- Is the employee untried or experienced?
- Can I expect this employee to produce favorable results?
- What can and should be delegated?
- How much training is needed with this particular delegated assignment?
- Whom would the assignment help to develop?
- Who can do it now?
- Who can be trained to do it?
- What is the employee's current workload and level of performance?

Criteria to Consider

The following questions and statements will help you analyze which employees might be best suited for which delegated assignments. Respond to each one, using examples from your current situation. Keep in mind the selection factors from the previous page as you work.

Does the work belong to a particular position?

Some tasks or projects fit right into existing work assignments and can logically be delegated there.

List two examples of such tasks from the past or two possibilities for the future, and where they would fit in well:

1. ____________________
2. ____________________

Who has the interest and/or the ability?

Analyze employee job performance periodically, and keep an inventory of the interests and abilities of your staff. Look for opportunities to give employees who are attending classes a chance to apply what they are learning.

Give consideration to interest as well as to ability. A minimally qualified person may take the assignment enthusiastically and develop the required skills; the best-qualified person with a low level of interest may do a poor job.

List two examples of such employee interests from the past or two prospects for the future:

1. ____________________
2. ____________________

Who will find the work challenging?

Studies reflect that large numbers of employees are unchallenged, and their boredom is reflected in their performance. Give them the pleasure of a new opportunity to achieve.

List two examples of employees you might want to challenge:

1. ____________________
2. ____________________

Whom will the assignment stretch and help to grow?

Some employees thrive on challenge and are willing to develop new skills to meet new job requirements. Give them the opportunity.

Identify two people in this category:

1. ______________________________

2. ______________________________

Who has been overlooked when you have delegated in the past?

Delegate to all of your employees and stretch them when you can. Avoid playing favorites or over-burdening some of your staff.

Delegating to an employee who has been untested in the past requires careful planning, but the payoff in added performance is potentially high.

An assignment delegated with care can bring a problem employee up to standard. An employee with unused potential can be motivated to new heights of achievement.

Every time you give an *unknown* the chance to perform in a new way, the overall depth, versatility, and morale of your unit will improve.

Identify two employees as possibilities for future delegation:

1. ______________________________

2. ______________________________

The exercise on the next page will test your skills at matching work assignments with the right employees.

CASE STUDY: Mix and Match

Five employees are described below along with 10 possible work assignments. Match the employee with the work assignment. Good luck!

Employee #1: Logan is an average employee. She is reliable and can be counted on to produce steady results. She seems bored at the routine of her work assignment but has not demonstrated any keen desire for a change, nor does she seem interested in improving her job performance. She is still learning some aspects of her job and needs to acquire a better understanding of the company's products.

Employee #2: Steve is eager and enthusiastic about his work. He constantly has ideas and suggestions for how to improve things. He spends a little too much time talking and entertaining others, but he gets his work done. His month-end report is a near disaster. As he says, "I'm just not very good with numbers." His supervisor feels that Steve needs to concentrate more on the details of his job, especially the month-end report.

Employee #3: Susan is new to the work unit. She is quiet and seems a little unsure of herself. Her work is satisfactory but she is reluctant to make decisions and exercise the authority of her job. So far she has not connected with the other employees well. She was a top performer in the new-hire orientation training.

Employee #4: Davis is the star of the group. He is on the ready now list for promotion and is awaiting an opening. Davis has strong leadership skills but can also manage the details of the job. His manager's only criticism is that Davis often keeps information to himself that should be shared with the rest of the employees. This behavior has caused some conflict within the work unit. His manager has cautioned him about his behavior, and Davis has promised to do better.

Employee #5: Zack has been in the work unit longer than anyone. He seems to lack motivation but knows the work thoroughly. He can be counted on to get his work done. His manager feels that Zack is an underachiever and has lost interest in his work because he has been doing it for so long. But because of his average performance, he does not qualify for a new assignment. He is stuck but he seems unwilling to do anything about it.

CONTINUED

CONTINUED

Below are the work assignments to be delegated to the above employees. Delegate each one by writing the employee's name next to the task. You may write in more than one employee's name for an assignment, and you may use an employee's name for more than one task, if you feel this is applicable.

	Work Assignments to Be Delegated	Delegated To
A.	Redesign the month-end employee report.	______________
B.	Train the employees on the new procedures.	______________
C.	Conduct new product research.	______________
D.	Lead a discussion on improving the work process.	______________
E.	Write a job description for HR to use.	______________
F.	Help design training for new employees.	______________
G.	Participate in the annual review with upper management.	______________
H.	Present a safety topic at the next staff meeting.	______________
I.	Summarize monthly reports for the unit.	______________
J.	Fill in as the acting supervisor.	______________

You probably found lots of possibilities for these assignments. Perhaps this exercise also made you think differently about some of your employees. If so, make notes for yourself here:

____

____

____

____

____

____

Check your answers with the author's suggested responses in the Appendix.

Delegating to Develop Employees

When delegating, managers often look for the perfect match of work assignment and employee ability—delegating to the strength of the individual. That is not always the best solution.

Remember, delegation serves three purposes:

- It allows the leader freedom to spend more time on planning, organizing, motivating, and controlling
- It provides different and often more interesting and challenging assignments for the employee
- It helps develop the individual

It is the third purpose—to develop the individual—that will help your employee grow in experience, which will enable both of you to move ahead in the organization and in your careers.

- When employees demonstrate they have considerable skill at particular work assignments, it may be best to provide them with something new and different. In this way they can develop new skills.
- When employees are new or struggling with their performance, it is usually a good idea to provide them with work assignments they can safely complete. This may help build their confidence.
- Before submitting employees for new assignments or promotions, make certain they have successfully completed a variety of assignments. These varied assignments may be your best argument for why your employee should get the new job.
- Keep in mind that most employees will respond favorably to increased responsibility. Make certain they get a chance.

The case study on the following page is an example of what can happen when managers fail to stretch their team members to take on new assignments.

CASE STUDY: Delegating for Individual Development

Megan is a conscientious and studious employee. Her supervisor Rich is preparing Megan for an advanced assignment. Since Megan is analytical and good with numbers, Rich usually assigns her reports and studies of an analytical nature. Of course, Megan excels at this type of work.

Meanwhile, Rich is also trying to develop Bill. Bill is outgoing and works well with people. Rich has been assigning Bill work that involves making presentations to the work unit and conducting meetings during Rich's absence. Bill excels at this type of work.

What do you think of Rich's developmental plans for Megan and Bill? Is Rich delegating the right kind of work? Suppose Bill and Megan are promoted and it turns out that Megan does not have good leadership skills, and Bill is not very good at analytical work.

What would you do if you were Rich? Why? What responsibility does Rich have in this case for the future development or failure of his employees?

In the space below write your response to these questions.

____

____

____

____

____

____

____

____

____

Compare your answers with the author's suggested responses in the Appendix.

This might be a good case study to discuss at your next management staff meeting, particularly if you have similar situations in your organization.

The delegation log on the next two pages will help you keep track of delegated assignments. Use it along with the worksheets in this section to help you do careful, detailed planning whenever you delegate.

DELEGATION

Work Assignment	Results Expected	Who Can Do It for Me Now?

Log

Who Can Be Trained to Do It?	Assigned To	Follow-Up Required

PART 4

Carrying Out the Delegation

Communicating the Delegation

The heart of the delegation process is the interaction between manager and employee when the assignment is made. Delegation is not just pushing work down. When you are delegating, you are consulting and developing as well as assigning work.

Open communication is vital. Success depends ultimately on the communication skills of the manager and the employee and the quality of their relationship. When there is a lack of trust on either side, or poor communication between them, the needed understanding and motivation are unlikely to be there.

When you are ready to hand off the assignment, face-to-face, two-way discussion is critical. It should end with employee commitment and assurance that the desired results will be achieved.

Agreement is an essential element of the conversation that takes place during the delegation hand-off. The employee must agree to accept the work and to meet the requirements of the assignment. The manager agrees to play a particular role during the assignment. The manager and employee essentially make a verbal contract that is clear, concise, and agreed upon. Always make certain that there is agreement.

Seven Steps in Delegating

The following steps are essential in communicating an assignment:

1. **Describe as fully as possible the project or task and the results expected.**

   Pass on all the information needed to get the job started, or let the employee know where it can be obtained. Indicate who else will be involved and describe their roles.

2. **Agree on standards of performance and timetables.**

   The scope of the assignment has already been determined, but you will want the employee's input on standards and a reasonable timetable for completion of the assignment.

3. **Determine any training or special help that will be needed, and when it will be provided.**

   Ask the individual to determine what support is needed for the successful completion of the assignment. Give the employee time to consider these needs before communicating them to you.

4. **Define the parameters and the resources, including budget, that will be available.**

   It is important to communicate the entire scope of the delegated work. Experienced team members will need less information, but others may need considerable detail to successfully complete the work.

5. **State the amount and frequency of feedback you expect.**

   Individual judgment comes into play here. If the employee is well prepared to take on the work assignment and can be fully trusted, then little feedback is needed. If the employee is new or otherwise untested, you will probably want to increase the frequency of feedback.

6. **Spell out the amount of authority being delegated.**

   This should be balanced according to the complexity of the task, your confidence in the employee, and your need to keep others informed.

   Selecting an appropriate level of authority is discussed later in this part.

7. **Tell others who is in charge.**

   It is important that you do not become a communications block between the delegatee and others who will be involved or affected.

Getting the Results You Expect

The manager has every right to expect results from the employee according to the parameters established when the delegation was made. Check (√) the expectations that your employees are currently satisfying when you delegate:

- ❑ Employees have a willing, can-do attitude and accept responsibility for the task.
- ❑ Employees ask questions and seek help when needed.
- ❑ You and others in the communications loop receive progress reports on time.
- ❑ The finished tasks are good examples of completed staff work.
- ❑ Employees use initiative and show dedication and commitment to the task.
- ❑ Time, money, equipment, and worker hours are seen as expensive resources and used accordingly.

If these expectations are to be met, employees must be prepared in advance, receive carefully planned delegations, be permitted to grow as the work is done, and be continually developed for increasingly important assignments.

Opportunities for Improvement

Think about times you have delegated tasks or projects and consider the seven steps in delegation. How does your process for delegating compare to those steps? Do you regularly include all the steps, or are there steps you have been missing? Are you getting what you expect?

Choose two examples of delegations you made recently, and answer the following questions for each one:

1. Briefly describe what you delegated and to whom:

   Example one: ______________________________

   ____

   ____

   Example two: ______________________________

   ____

   ____

2. What did you do in communicating each delegation that worked well?

   Example one: ______________________________

   ____

   ____

   Example two: ______________________________

   ____

   ____

3. What opportunities for improvement can you see in how you communicated each delegation?

   Example one: ______________________________

   ____

   ____

   Example two: ______________________________

   ____

   ____

Six Levels of Authority

An important element in getting the results you expect is delegating the right amount of authority, considering the task, the circumstances, and the employee's ability. Some managers do not delegate any authority because they want full personal control. Others give full authority because they want to be free of the task. Most of the time, something in between these two extremes will work best.

What level of control do you most frequently delegate? Could you stretch your comfort zone, free yourself of more of the work, and further develop your employees? Or do you need to pay attention to those employees for whom less authority may be appropriate?

Before you make your next delegation, review the delegation levels described on the next page.

Six Levels of Authority

Level of Authority	Assignment	Reason
1	Look into the situation. Get all the facts and report them to me. I'll decide what to do.	The employee is new to the job and the manager wants to retain control of the outcome.
2	Identify the problem. Determine alternative solutions and the pluses and minuses of each. Recommend one for my approval.	The employee is being developed and the manager wants to see how he or she approaches problems and makes decisions.
3	Examine the issues. Let me know what you intend to do, but don't take action until you check with me.	The manager has confidence in the employee, but does not want action taken without his or her approval. This may be because of constraints from higher management, or the need to communicate the action to others before it is taken.
4	Solve the problem. Let me know what you intend to do, then do it, unless I say not to.	The manager has confidence in the employee's ability and judgment, and only wants a final check before action is taken.
5	Take action on this matter, and let me know what you did.	The manager has full confidence in the employee, has no need to be consulted, and wants to know only the outcome.
6	Take action. No further contact with me is necessary.	The supervisor has total confidence in the employee. The employee has full authority to act and does not need to report the results back to the manager.

Teaching Problem-Solving Techniques

Solving problems is an ongoing experience in all organizations. When managers choose levels of authority for delegation, the level of problem-solving authority is important. It is important to clarify up front who is going to make decisions related to problem solving. Ideally the delegatee will make the decision but that is not always practical or wise. At least the employee who does the work should be allowed to participate in the problem-solving process.

Many managers spend too much time solving problems that should be handled by the employees they supervise. When managers try to solve all the problems, team members feel less empowered, can become frustrated, and feel their personal growth is limited. The manager ends up with less time to plan, organize, motivate, and control.

Delegation is more effective when the manager participates in problem solving only when necessary, instead of dominating it. In view of this, problem solving should be taught at every level of the organization. Some employees make quality decisions instinctually while most of us need some experience and training to get it right.

Seven Steps to Solving Problems

The problem-solving process varies in its level of complexity. Sometimes the solution is simple and straightforward, while at other times solutions produce new problems to solve. One basic approach is outlined below. Check (√) those steps that would be useful in your operation:

❑ **STEP 1—State what appears to be the problem.**

The real problem may not surface until facts have been gathered and analyzed. Therefore, start with a supposition that can later be confirmed or corrected.

❑ **STEP 2—Gather facts, feelings, and opinions.**

What happened? Where, when, and how did it occur? What is its size, scope, and severity? Who and what is affected? Is it likely to happen again? Does it need to be corrected? Time and expense may require problem solvers to think through what they need and assign priorities to the more critical elements.

❑ **STEP 3—Restate the problem.**

The facts help make this possible and provide supporting data. The actual problem may or may not be the same as stated in Step 1.

❑ **STEP 4—Identify alternative solutions.**

Generate ideas. Do not eliminate any possible solutions until several have been discussed.

❑ **STEP 5—Evaluate alternatives.**

Which will provide the optimum solution? What are the risks? Are the costs in keeping with the benefits? Will the solution create new problems?

❑ **STEP 6—Implement the decision.**

Who must be involved? To what extent? How, when, and where? Whom will the decision affect? What might go wrong? How will results be reported and verified?

❑ **STEP 7—Evaluate the results.**

Test the solution against the desired results. Modify the solution if better results are needed.

CASE STUDY: The Parking Lot Case

Often determining the problem is rather easy but finding the cause of the problem can be more difficult. This case study illustrates how important finding the cause can be. It also indicates some problems in the delegation process.

The Ace Fitness Club had a shortage of parking places for its members. During peak hours, the parking lot was full and many members had to park on the street. The city passed a new ordinance that restricted the street parking because of neighbors' complaints. The ordinance was to be effective in 30 days.

Alex was assigned the task of solving the problem. He started by observing how many members had to park on nearby streets when the parking lot was full. He found that during peak hours the club was short an average of 20 parking spaces.

The Solution: Alongside the club is a picnic area used for special events and member parties. Alex determined the picnic area could be turned into a parking lot with 40 spaces at a cost of $200,000. He presented the idea to upper management and they told him to proceed. Alex knew his biggest problem was going to be telling the members that the picnic area was coming down. But he also knew the members would be happy about the additional parking. Alex announced his solution to the parking problem in the club's newsletter.

It appears Alex has solved the parking problem, but has he found and solved the cause of the problem?

A New Problem: Upon hearing that the picnic area is going to be destroyed for a parking lot, the members are outraged.

Alex calls a meeting of the membership and nearly 200 people show up. He explains the reasoning behind tearing down the picnic area. One member tells Alex: "Change the club's guest policy. That might fix the problem." Several other members offer their support of changing the guest policy. Alex isn't sure what the guest policy is, so he promises the group he will look into it.

On further investigation, Alex learns that guests are free the first week of every month and they pay only $3 for additional visits. Other clubs are charging $15 per guest visit. He further learns that this policy was put into effect when the club was new, as a way to attract new members.

CONTINUED

CONTINUED

Alex studies the issue and then goes back to management and explains the problem. The free guest days are eliminated and the guest fees are raised to $15. Now, during peak hours, there is plenty of parking in the club parking lot, the members still have their picnic area, and the club doesn't have to spend $200,000.

In this case, Alex initially solved the problem but he failed to look at other factors. He simply saw it as a shortage of parking places. Whenever you set out to solve a problem, or whenever you delegate a problem to an employee, keep this case in mind. Finding the cause of the problem leads to a real solution.

Alex did not pay attention to the complete problem-solving process. What steps did he miss?

____

____

____

____

____

If you were Alex's manager, what might you have done in the delegation process that would help Alex avoid the problems he ran into?

____

____

____

____

____

CONTINUED

Compare your answers with the author's suggested responses in the Appendix.

There are times when a solution can cause another problem. In Alex's case the members were upset because he was going to tear down the picnic area. Suppose the destruction of the picnic area was the right solution for the fitness club. Then a new problem would need to be resolved: members who were upset, with no simple solution available. The next case study will look at what happens when problems continue to arise.

CASE STUDY: One Problem After Another

The more complex the problem-solving effort, the more likely it is that new problems will arise. Remember the story about the man who set out to drain the swamp and wound up fighting alligators? The swamp story is a good example of one problem leading to another problem. Sometimes the problems can seem nearly endless. Here is an example of such a situation. See how many problems you can find that need to be solved, and consider what could be done differently in the delegation process.

Salma was assigned to coach a new girls' basketball team in the school where she works. The season was going to start in three weeks. Salma thought her biggest problem was to get enough girls signed up. She worked hard at recruiting and was successful in getting 15 girls to sign up. Now she needed a place to practice—open time in the school gym was scarce. Another local gym was available but there was a fee of $10 per day for its use. The school told her it couldn't afford the $10-a-day gym fee. Salma would have to hold practice in the school gym when it was available, which was in the evenings. Two girls said they couldn't attend practices in the evening.

The team also needed uniforms. Half of the games were away games, and Salma didn't know how she was going to handle transportation. Salma held her first practice but realized she didn't have enough basketballs. Next, her best player said she could attend practice only one day a week. Then one of the parents complained that Salma was working the girls too hard during practice. Just before the first game, Salma learned the uniforms wouldn't be ready in time. The supplier also demanded payment. In spite of it all, Salma's team won their first game.

CONTINUED

CONTINUED

How many problems?

Salma set out to form a basketball team. She thought her biggest problem was getting enough girls to sign up. But one problem led to another. In the space below make a list of her problems.

1. Getting enough girls to sign up.
2. __________
3. __________
4. __________
5. __________
6. __________
7. __________
8. __________
9. __________
10. __________
11. __________
12. __________
13. __________

If you were the one who gave Salma this assignment, what could you have done to develop Salma's problem-solving skills?

____

____

What could you have done related to Salma's level of authority?

____

____

Compare your answers with the author's suggested responses in the Appendix.

Following Through

The goal in delegation is satisfactory completion of the assigned task or project through the personal efforts of those handling the work. It is important that the manager follow through with any support, resources, or information promised. A feedback mechanism, suitable to the situation, is an important part of this follow-through. All these considerations should be discussed when you make the delegation.

THE ESSENTIAL ELEMENTS OF FOLLOW-THROUGH		
The Manager's Role	**The Manager's Communication**	**The Manager's Action**
Encourage independence Allow freedom of action in keeping with the level of delegation Support initiative and creativity Share opinions and show interest Accept mistakes and learn from them Provide training when needed Live with differences as long as objectives are met Be available Do not take the job back unless absolutely essential (coach through problems)	Share all pertinent information Do not become a communications block between the employee and the others involved Monitor progress, but do not hover Provide honest feedback Insist that your need to know be fulfilled on time	Assess results Suggest course corrections if appropriate and unrecognized by those handling tasks Help solve problems, but only those that are beyond the employee's ability to handle Evaluate performance Plan any needed training for the future Compliment efforts and reward success

CASE STUDY: Poor Work by Competent Employees

Marla is the manager of an insurance company claims group. Her employees are well trained and several have considerable experience in claims work. Much of the work is routine, but occasionally an unusual claim is submitted that requires a great deal of investigation.

When this occurs, Marla assigns one of her claims representatives to the case. She delegates the authority necessary for that person to gather the facts, develop alternative solutions, and recommend the action to be taken. But Marla always makes the final decision.

Often these unusual claims are for high dollar amounts. As a result, upper management wants status reports. Marla always handles these status reports personally. Marla also acts as the point of contact when people outside the company are providing pertinent data regarding these unusual claims. She passes the data onto her representatives and tells them how to act upon it.

Marla has been disappointed with the way her employees have handled most of these claims. She feels they are not giving their best effort. She has had several discussions with her staff about this situation, but she hasn't found a solution.

Answer *T* for *True* or *F* for *False* for the following questions regarding Marla's delegation.

1. ___ Marla delegates the same level of authority to each subordinate.
2. ___ Marla hands off each unusual claim in the same manner.
3. ___ Marla probably spends too much time on tasks that her subordinates should be performing.
4. ___ Marla controls the key elements of the claim investigation.
5. ___ Marla keeps the upper management recognition for herself.
6. ___ Marla doesn't trust her representatives.
7. ___ Marla is too controlling in the way she hands off aspects of the claims work.

Compare your answers to the author's responses in the Appendix.

After completing this case study, are there any delegation hand-off techniques of your own that you want to change or improve? Make notes for yourself below.

___

___

Solving Delegation Problems

It is unreasonable to expect that all of your work assignment delegation will go smoothly. Doing everything right during the delegation process still does not guarantee success. There are always variables, and the biggest one of all is the employee.

While most employees want responsibility, a few do not. While most keep their promises, some do not. When you are unsure of the employee, increased feedback and monitoring may be needed. As the employee becomes more responsible and skilled, the monitoring can be reduced.

Sometimes an employee cannot break the cycle of having the manager continually help and make decisions. In this situation, the employee never seems to gain much ground and is constantly kept from failing by the manager. When the delegated work is not the most urgent, perhaps it is okay to allow this type of employee to fail in order to teach a valuable lesson. The key to such situations is your good judgment.

The case study on the next page illustrates how you might approach this type of problem.

CASE STUDY: The Reluctant Employee

On two occasions, Saul delegated nearly identical special projects to Petra. His purpose was to develop Petra's project management skills. On the first project, Saul worked closely with Petra and helped her nearly every step of the way. On the second project, he tried to monitor only Petra's progress but she kept pulling him back into the mix.

Saul has a third project he is going to delegate to Petra. This time he is determined that she will complete the project on her own with only modest help from him. Although the project is important, there is plenty of time to correct any mistakes Petra might make.

Petra starts on the third project and immediately asks for help. Saul listens to Petra's concerns and tells her to use her best judgment. Petra continues the project but again she asks Saul for help. Saul tells Petra that the problem she's having is similar to the last project he gave her and she needs to take similar action. The due date is approaching and Petra isn't very close to completing the project. Once again she asks Saul for help with some decisions she must make. Again Saul tells her to use her best judgment.

On the due date Petra hands in the completed project. Saul reviews it with her and decides that she did a good job. He especially liked the decisions she made as part of the project. He congratulates her. Petra feels very good about her work.

Summary:

Petra made some valuable progress because her supervisor was willing to let her fail. Saul pushed Petra to make her own decisions and to complete the delegated work without assistance. This was a win-win result for everyone.

Here is an important question for you. Suppose Petra did not complete the project in a satisfactory manner? As Petra's supervisor, what would you do next? Assume Petra's regular work is satisfactory. Write your answer here.

____

____

Compare your answer with the author's suggested response in the Appendix.

A team member's lack of skill or confidence is only one of several problems you might encounter in delegation. The chart starting on the next page provides a simple guide to identifying and solving other potential problems and delegation. Some problems are caused by employees, some by managers. As you read, you may wish to note those problems you most frequently have, and how you can change the situation.

Delegator's Troubleshooting Guide

Possible Problems	Possible Solutions
1. Manager delegates only meaningless chores.	Delegating only meaningless chores creates resentment. Mix in some of your favorite things and share the good times.
2. Employees resist the work, claiming they don't know how to do it.	Provide training as necessary, or break down the job and let them handle as many components as they can. Add more as they learn.
3. Employees say they are too busy.	First verify their workloads. If it is true, consider giving the task to others.
4. The task is repetitive, but it would take you longer to delegate the job than to do it yourself.	Get smart. At least have someone start to learn the process. Soon that team member will be doing it all. Otherwise you will still be doing it next year.
5. "Upper management requires me to sign these invoices and other basic documents, like shipping and receiving papers."	Ask management to change the policy so that employees closer to the work can sign. You are probably already taking the employees' word that it is all right to sign off.
6. "Poor results on this project will make me look bad."	Your job is to let employees develop by taking on new endeavors. They may make some mistakes, but they will learn from them. You can minimize serious mistakes by using an appropriate level of delegation and by monitoring.
7. "If my employees can do the tough jobs well, I'm not needed."	Organizations desperately need managers who can get superior performance from employees.

Possible Problems	Possible Solutions
8. "My own manager expects me to do this personally."	If that is the case, you had better do it, but first check it out—your manager may just want to be sure you see that it gets done.
9. "I'll lose my skills if I delegate too much of the work."	Managers need to learn to manage. They need to teach their employees the work skills.
10. "If I delegate all my work, I won't have anything to do."	Direct your attention to planning, organizing, motivating, and controlling. There is plenty to do.
11. "I don't understand the work well enough to control it or make a judgment about how well it is being done."	Learn enough about unfamiliar areas, ask the right questions, and assess the answers.
12. Employees with delegated tasks keep coming back for advice and help.	Whenever employees ask how you would do the task, turn it around and ask how they would do it. Reinforce correct answers warmly. If you feel sure they can handle the problem, or the consequences of an error are low, be unavailable. Help them build confidence.
13. Some employees are overburdened and others don't have enough to do.	You are overdelegating to those who are most trusted, and failing to develop those in whom you lack confidence. It is essential to raise the confidence level by giving everyone a chance to perform.

Possible Problems	Possible Solutions
14. Employees do not understand organizational objectives and standards.	Tell the employees what is at stake and the "why" of the job. As often as you can, involve the employees in setting objectives and standards.
15. "Employees don't do things the way I do."	Concentrate on getting the right results and learn to live with differences. You may even learn something new.
16. The manager delegates either everything or nothing.	Study the six levels of delegation described earlier in this part and learn to apply them.
17. The manager assigns the least challenging work to the most qualified people.	This is sometimes needed, but you may be doing it because you fear mistakes. Select a level of delegation that fits the employee and the situation. Some mistakes will occur; they will provide learning experiences. It is a serious mistake to burn out your best people.
18. The manager and the employee have trouble agreeing on the specifics of the delegation.	Review and clarify objectives to be sure they are understood. Delegate accordingly. Do not be a nitpicker. Follow up as necessary to see that the right results are obtained.
19. The employee's performance is jeopardizing a successful outcome.	Identify the reason and take corrective action. This might include changing the level of authority and providing more support. Acting carelessly could shatter the employee's confidence.
20. Deadlines are not being met.	Reassess objectives, standards, and priorities with the employee. Identify the reasons for missed deadlines and take corrective action.

Monitoring Progress to Ensure Success

From the Delegator's Troubleshooting Guide, you can see that many problems can occur when you delegate. One of the most common problems—managers' concern about poor results reflecting on them—warrants more examination. This is a legitimate concern.

When employees fail, the manager is often the one who has to explain. And poor results by the employee do reflect on the manager. These realities keep many leaders from seriously delegating assignments. They simply don't want to take the chance.

But the development of people is crucial to the success of the organization, and delegation plays a key role in that development. Managers must accept this responsibility along with the responsibility for successful work completion. To meet both responsibilities, managers must keep in mind that an important part of the management process is controlling. A key question to ask yourself with every delegated work assignment is, to what degree am I going to monitor?

The question is not *whether* you are going to monitor, but how and to what degree. You must always monitor because that is the only way you can head off problems, and a simple monitoring plan can keep you informed every step of the way. The exception, as shown in The Reluctant Employee case study, is when you are willing to let the employees succeed or fail on their own.

Successful leaders have learned how to balance the amount of monitoring they do. Read the following case study as an illustration of this fact.

CASE STUDY: Different Plans for Different Employees

John is meeting with his manager, Crawford. The purpose of the meeting is to discuss the work of John's direct reports. Crawford wants to make certain that they are all getting a fair chance at developing their skills. At this point in their meeting, they are talking about Ken:

John: Ken is my best performer. He knows his job well. I have delegated several key assignments to him and he has been successful in each one. He has good organizational and people skills, and I think he's ready for promotion.

Crawford: That's a big step. What work have you delegated to him?

John: The most important thing he's done is fill in for me as the acting manager for two weeks when I was on vacation, and for a week when I was off site for training. Each time he managed the unit well and showed good leadership. When I was on vacation, he handled the back-order situation without going to you or another manager for help. He saved us a lot of time and money by his quick actions.

Crawford: I remember that. He did do a good job in that situation. You must have given him complete authority to do your job while you were gone.

John: I did. I trust him completely, and whenever I delegate to him I barely monitor what's he doing.

Crawford: Is that wise?

John: Yes, it is. He has earned my trust and he is always reliable. When we do the evaluations next month I'm going to rate him as outstanding.

Crawford: How about Nan? What's going on with her?

John: She is still struggling—especially with the technical part of things. I have to monitor her closely.

Crawford: Have you delegated any special assignments to her?

John: She has handled three assignments involving technical training and she was poor at each one. I had to monitor closely and on the last one I had to bail her out.

Crawford: What do you have her working on now?

John: Just her regular job. That's about all she can handle right now. If in the future she learns the technical side, I can think about delegating to her.

Crawford: So you don't have a developmental plan for her?

CONTINUED

CONTINUED

John: The plan is for her to learn her job. Then and only then can we think about development beyond that.

Crawford: Do you think it's smart to keep added work assignments from her?

John: At this time, yes. She needs to concentrate on learning her basic job.

Crawford: Is she still worth a rating of satisfactory?

John: No. I'm planning on giving her an unsatisfactory rating.

Crawford: That's pretty serious. Keep me informed on her performance. How is Anna doing?

John: She's coming along pretty well. I've just finished giving her a tough assignment. Although I had to help her here and there, she performed well. She is going to be working on the problems with production and I'm going to let her run with it. I plan to get involved only if needed.

Crawford: So she still needs monitoring.

John: Not as much as before. I think she may have turned the corner. We'll see how she does on this production assignment. I am pleased with her progress and I still think she may have considerable potential.

Crawford: I like the way you're staying involved with each one of your people.

John seems to have different plans for each employee. Ken is given considerable latitude and authority to complete assignments, while Nan is currently just focusing on her job as John monitors her closely. Meanwhile Anna is making progress and John is reducing the level of monitoring on her assignments.

Observations about monitoring from this case study:

- John's level of monitoring is different for each employee
- John is willing to reduce or increase his monitoring based on his subordinate's job performance
- John always monitors
- John monitors as a way to head off problems

CONTINUED

CONTINUED

Delegation is an essential part of the management process. Good leaders monitor their employees' progress in delegated assignments and adjust their approach according to each employee's skills and needs. Appropriate monitoring is an opportunity to demonstrate your flexibility.

The situations you face as a manager may be more difficult and more complex than the ones in this case study. Answer the questions below to help you think about your own specific situation:

Consider a monitoring process that worked well for you. Why was it successful for that particular employee?

____

____

____

____

____

Consider a monitoring situation that did not work well for you, or is not working well currently. What could you do to change that particular situation?

____

____

____

____

____

PART 5

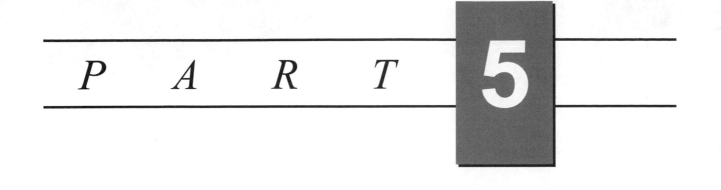

Using Delegation for Managing Change

Change Requires Smooth Transitions

In some organizations the word *change* itself is enough to produce strong emotional reactions. There are those who fear it, those who misunderstand its purpose, and those who thrive on it.

Change is actually healthy and positive when it is well planned and when those who are affected by it are committed to the objectives it is designed to achieve. With effective planning and realistic commitment, change tends to stabilize conditions rather than upset them. A positive change process keeps the organization in touch with the changing realities of the marketplace rather than on a comfortable road to disaster.

One of the key skills in management is introducing change and overcoming the resistance that may impede a smooth transition. Unfortunately, managers in recent years have often been caught in a whirlpool of change that has diminished their financial resources, reduced their staff, cut their training budget, and increased their personal workload. They have witnessed, and often had to preside over, the elimination of layers of management and staff, often including friends and trusted associates. Not all these changes have been well planned, and in many cases chaos rather than efficiency has reigned. Transitions have been anything but smooth.

When transitional issues negatively affect productivity, profitability, and customer satisfaction, managers are expected to overcome obstacles and solve the problems. During such times, it is often possible to use delegation techniques to inform employees, permit direct participation in transitional activities, reduce anxieties, and focus their attention on meaningful goals.

Understanding Resistance to Change

Using delegation to facilitate change requires an understanding of the initial impact change has on organizations and their people. Changes occur for many reasons, including new technology, a need for new systems, or the belief that a change in the organization's structure will improve its efficiency or profitability.

In nearly all cases, employees are the first to feel the impact of change. Suddenly there is uncertainty, and the simple fact that people resist change comes into play. Most of us like to stay in our comfort zones and it is natural to resist change.

This resistance is just part of human nature. Research suggests a number of reasons for it. Check (√) those in the list below that you have seen in organizations where you have worked.

- ❑ The fear of failure in a different environment
- ❑ The objective of the change is not clear
- ❑ Persons affected by the change are not involved in the planning
- ❑ Communication about the change is poor
- ❑ Anxiety over job security goes unrelieved
- ❑ There is high satisfaction with the status quo
- ❑ The change is too rapid
- ❑ The personal costs are too high compared to the rewards
- ❑ The needs of the work group are ignored

Some drama is associated with any change—drama that feeds on half-truths, gossip, and negativity. Leaders must do what they can to defuse this drama. They must help others through the change, even when the purpose and outcome are uncertain. This can be an ideal time for delegation.

Adjusting Your Approach

Your own approaches to delegation, including how you communicate, how you approach change, and how you focus on goals, are critical in leading your employees through change. How you delegate during a change process can make a major difference in the impact of the change on your employees and their work.

Check (√) the statements that describe you, and plan to develop skills that can make you a more effective leader in times of change.

Success-Centered Delegator	Doubt-Centered Delegator
❑ Concentrates on successful results and high goals	❑ Focuses on and transmits fear of failure; sets fail-safe goals
❑ Reinforces employees' strengths and abilities; confident of success.	❑ Expresses grave doubts about employees' abilities and limits, or arbitrarily reduces authority
❑ Encourages employee participation in setting goals and objectives	❑ Personally sets arbitrary goals and objectives
❑ Readily accepts new ideas and creative solutions	❑ Discourages anything new or untried
❑ Communicates freely and openly, holding nothing back	❑ Withholds information that is difficult to communicate
❑ Recognizes achievement and reinforces it	❑ Doesn't recognize success until it is endorsed from above
❑ Looks at the implications of each assignment for the future and assigns tasks accordingly	❑ Focuses on short-range goals and discourages employees who see implications for the future
❑ Encourages employees to appraise their performance and suggest improvements	❑ Tells people what went wrong and what to do about it.

Focusing Employee Efforts

In a changing environment, the leader has to work harder to set a climate for effective performance. A focus of employee efforts is required to provide an atmosphere in which employees can find definitions of their work, the organization's goals, a future they can believe in, and direction for their own career. You can begin this process by concentrating employee concerns on their work group and what it should be doing. Begin by:

- Thinking through and articulating for yourself where the group is going in terms of what you believe to be organizational objectives. Specifically, what will be the role of the group and what will it look like after the change is implemented?
- Sharing that vision with employees and talking through their concerns.
- Asking employees to join you in designing a bridge that will take the group from where it is now to where employees envision it being. Identify tasks that will have to be performed and obstacles that will have to be overcome. Set meaningful goals.

Determine how tasks and responsibilities can be defined and delegated to individuals for accomplishment. Schedule periodic meetings to permit employees to share individual progress and pool ideas to facilitate the change process. You can transform unfocused, uninformed, non-participating, complaining, anxious employees into responsible stakeholders once they realize they can make a direct contribution to the organization's transition.

The case study on the next page is an excellent example of a manager taking action by using delegation effectively to overcome obstacles during change.

CASE STUDY: Rumors of Change

Marlon supervised 14 workers who were part of the production group. Their responsibility included final testing of consumer products, followed by packaging and then delivery to the warehouse where the products were placed in inventory. Consumer product sales for this quarter were off by nearly 20% and as a result the inventory levels were too high. When a similar situation occurred three years ago, there had been a reorganization of the production group. Twenty percent of the production workers were assigned to other groups and a few were laid off.

The rumors of another reorganization were running rampant throughout the production group. Marlon discussed the situation with his manager and received assurances that there were no plans for a reorganization. He shared this information with his team members; but the rumors and drama persisted, productivity slowed, and morale slipped. Marlon decided to take action.

He knew the circumstances three years ago were vastly different from the current situation. He met with three of his strongest performers and asked them to take on an interesting assignment. They were to research the company's financial health and overall situation of three years ago and contrast it with today's. At first the three were hesitant, but Marlon promised to guide them through the assignment. They would have to keep up their other work, but the high inventory levels had provided times when their work was slower, and these three were usually ready for challenges. They started working.

In a short time, the three employees had completed their assignment. Marlon had them present their findings to the team. The three addressed the rumors that were circulating and dispelled each one. They showed how the company was more profitable today because of the reorganization of three years ago. They pointed out to the group that although consumer product sales were off, overall company-wide sales were up. Their presentation was so successful they were asked to present it to other production group work units.

Marlon told his manager that he could have presented the same set of facts, but when it came from the team members, there was immediate acceptance. He was also able to report that productivity was back up and most of the rumors and drama had died out. And he added, "My three employees learned a lot."

Marlon successfully got his work unit back on track. Although his delegation was different from the norm, it worked and his employees learned from it.

Let's finish this part with one more case study. In this case the manager is faced with cutting expenses and that may realistically mean layoffs. Read the case and decide what you might do in a similar circumstance.

CASE STUDY: Implementing Change

Terence is the purchasing manager for New Concepts, a medium-size computer software company. Senior management announced last week that the company was restructuring to cut costs and improve its standing in the marketplace. A number of changes will be made in internal and external procedures throughout the company. The changes were a complete surprise to Terence and other managers at his level, who had not been consulted.

A thick binder is distributed to each manager. It contains the new business plan for the company. In it, specific goals and objectives for the organization are clarified. Terence sees that he will have to reduce his operating budget by 10%. There is no mention of layoffs in the plan. Guidelines for this transition are pretty sketchy.

Purchasing employees are worried what the cut in their budget will mean to them. The drama they engage in centers around key issues and legitimate concerns. Will the budget cut mean layoffs? A freeze on wages? Elimination of overtime pay? A freeze on promotions or transfers? An increase in the employee cost of medical insurance? Suspension of the 401(k) plan? Shorter work hours? A cut in year-end profit-sharing bonuses? A cut in other employee benefits? Reassignment to other groups? Terence is also concerned about his own future.

Rumors swirl and productivity slows. It is obvious that the organization cannot tolerate the drain on productivity and the negative attitudes being displayed. Terence decides to involve his group in deciding how to reduce the department's budget by 10%. He announces that they will jointly develop a plan. But he is uncertain as to how to proceed.

How would you delegate this issue to your team members? Would you set up a committee with yourself as the head? Would you involve all your employees? Would you have them compete against one another? What ideas do you have for delegating this important issue? Write your answer here.

____

____

____

____

____

Compare your answers with the author's suggested responses in the Appendix.

APPENDIX

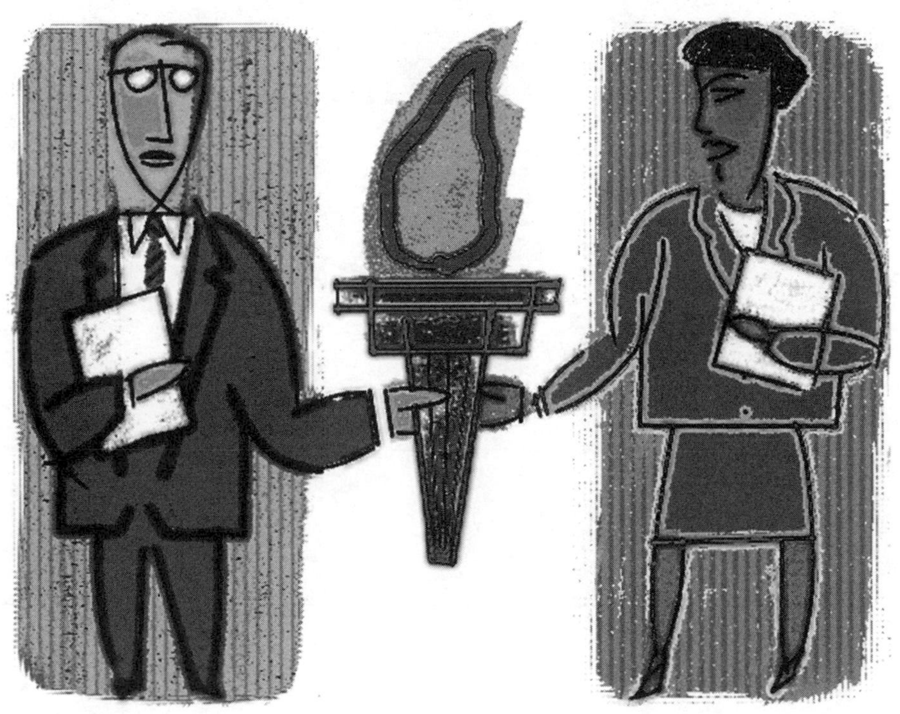

Making Employee Commitment Possible

Managers cannot do it all, no matter how talented and committed they may be. Their success is measured by their ability to delegate intelligently and then motivate employees to accomplish the goals of the organization. The highest level of achievement is attained when a team is committed to the task and full use is made of each member's talents.

Commitment cannot be forced. It is self-generating and usually develops through a feeling of empowerment. People increase their commitment to a team when they are allowed to contribute to its success. Once employees are actively involved in delegated projects and activities, including problem solving, they develop a sense of ownership. People feel more important and needed when they share a responsibility for results. Employees contribute their best to problem solving when they have a personal stake in doing so.

As a manager, you control the degree to which your employees are involved. Open up opportunities for participation through delegation, and watch the commitment grow.

In the following pages, you will measure your progress in what you have learned about delegation and prepare an action plan for yourself.

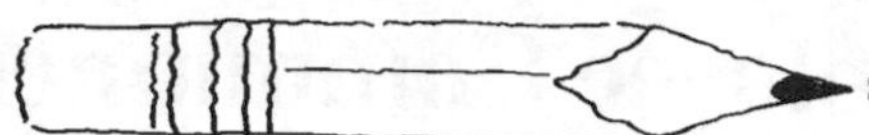

REVIEW

For each of the following statements, indicate whether you believe it to be true or false.

True	False		
❑	❑	1.	Most managers excel at delegation.
❑	❑	2.	Delegation is an indispensable management skill.
❑	❑	3.	It is all right to delegate tasks you dislike.
❑	❑	4.	Delegation is essential to the development of employees and the improvement of productivity.
❑	❑	5.	Employees appreciate your intervention in their decision-making.
❑	❑	6.	The list of tasks a manager cannot delegate is quite long.
❑	❑	7.	Employees dislike managers who delegate.
❑	❑	8.	As you move up, you must learn to delegate operating tasks you once performed yourself.
❑	❑	9.	Delegation is one way to use and reinforce creative talents.
❑	❑	10.	Managers must always keep key results areas in mind when delegating.
❑	❑	11.	Delegation is a positive act and requires very little thought or preparation.
❑	❑	12.	You do not really know what people can do until you give them a chance under the proper conditions.
❑	❑	13.	All delegated work should be handed off in the same manner with the same degree of instruction.
❑	❑	14.	The heart of the delegation process is the interaction between the manager and the employee when the assignment is communicated.

CONTINUED

CONTINUED

True	False	
❑	❑	15. A common management mistake is failing to delegate authority commensurate with the task.
❑	❑	16. The goal in delegation is the satisfactory completion of the assigned task through the personal efforts of those assigned the task.
❑	❑	17. Teaching employees to solve problems helps prepare them for delegation.
❑	❑	18. Any time you perform a task someone else could do, you keep yourself from a task only you can do.

Compare your answers with the author's suggested responses in the Appendix

Ten Traps to Avoid

You can further develop your delegation skills by being aware of the traps to avoid. This list will help you focus on the ones that you specifically want to identify and change.

Check (√) those you feel you most need to avoid.

- ❑ 1. Thinking you can do everything yourself
- ❑ 2. Failing to give employees challenging assignments with enough latitude to handle them
- ❑ 3. Carelessly selecting an authority level when assigning a project
- ❑ 4. Overlooking delegation opportunities for untried and untested employees
- ❑ 5. Holding on to non-management tasks that someone else could do
- ❑ 6. Using too little or too much follow-up
- ❑ 7. Withholding vital information pertinent to a delegated assignment
- ❑ 8. Failing to recognize employee accomplishments
- ❑ 9. Overburdening your best, most trusted people because you have not prepared anyone else
- ❑ 10. Failing to hold a critique with an employee after the accomplishment of a major task to see what you both have learned

A Delegation Checklist

The following checklist is designed to guide managers through the delegation process. Use it as a tool to help you plan effective delegations.

1. **Personal Preparation**

   I have reviewed my job and analyzed or identified:

   _____ My duties and responsibilities
   _____ Key results areas
   _____ Objectives
   _____ Management tasks vs. operating work
   _____ The assignments I can delegate

2. **Planning the Delegation**

   I have planned the delegation and established or considered:

   _____ The objectives to be accomplished
   _____ Completion dates
   _____ Standards to be met
   _____ The decision-making required
   _____ The amount of authority to be delegated
   _____ Budget and other resource requirements
   _____ How involved I want to be
   _____ What feedback I want and when I want it

3. **Selecting the Right Person**

   I have selected an employee after considering:

   _____ To whom the work logically belongs
   _____ Who has the interest or the ability
   _____ Who will find the work challenging
   _____ Whom the assignment will help to develop
   _____ Who has been overlooked in the past
   _____ Who is best qualified
   _____ Who has the time
   _____ Who will do the best job

4. **Making the Delegation**

When I communicate the delegation I will:

_____ Describe the task and the results expected
_____ Agree on standards of performance and timetables
_____ Determine training needs and when training will be provided
_____ State the amount and frequency of feedback I expect
_____ Define parameters and resources, including budgets
_____ Spell out the level of authority
_____ Tell others who is in charge

5. **Following Through**

I will follow through by:

_____ Setting reasonable reporting and review schedules
_____ Respecting the level of delegation given
_____ Communicating freely and openly
_____ Supporting the employee to the extent required
_____ Offering encouragement and reinforcing employee strengths and abilities
_____ Recognizing achievement
_____ Intervening only if absolutely necessary

Developing a Personal Action Plan

Think over the material you have read. Review the self-analysis questionnaires and the Missed Opportunities page. Rethink the case studies and the reinforcement exercises. What have you learned about delegation? What have you learned about yourself as a delegator? How can you apply what you have learned? Make a commitment to yourself to become a better delegator and a more effective leader by designing a personal action plan to help you accomplish this goal.

The following guide may help you clarify your goals and outline the actions required to achieve them.

1. My current delegation skills are effective in the following areas:

   ____

   ____

2. I need to improve my delegation skills in the following areas:

   ____

   ____

3. My goals for improving my delegation skills are as follows (be sure they are specific, attainable, and measurable):

   ____

   ____

4. These people are resources who can help me achieve my goals:

   ____

   ____

5. Following are my action steps, along with a timetable to accomplish each goal:

   ____

   ____

   ____

   ____

   ____

   ____

   ____

   ____

Appendix to Part 1

Comments & Suggested Responses

Case Study: Involving Employees in Planning

There are several possible answers to this case study. Much depends on the employee's abilities, the work environment, and various other factors. Here's one answer that will work.

The task is the completion of element #3: Formulate and establish polices and procedures. Since Kim and Stuart are strong performers, they should be assigned a leadership role and each could have responsibility for a group of employees. They should meet with their group to formulate policies and procedures. Receiving feedback is a matter of choice. To keep all subordinates involved, the manager might meet with each group and hear their findings.

The employees will feel more involved. The manager's role during this process is crucial. If the manager is too active, the employees may feel that not much has been delegated. If the manager remains too distant, the groups could flounder and not be able to correct mistakes in time. The best approach is for the manager to monitor progress by checking with the group leaders periodically.

Motivating True-False Exercise

1. False
2. True
3. True
4. True
5. False
6. True
7. True
8. True

Controlling True-False Exercise

1. True
2. False
3. True
4. True
5. False
6. True

Case Study: The Sales Funnel

To produce the desired sales, three activities must be controlled:

- Each salesperson must make 30 customer telephone calls
- Each salesperson must make 10 customer appointments
- Each salesperson must make 10 presentations per week

If these three activities occur, then two sales should be made. The desired result is produced by controlling the activities that lead to sales. It is called a sales funnel because the 30 customer telephone calls are placed in the wide mouth of the funnel and two sales come out the narrow tube end of the funnel.

Case Study: The-Do-It Yourself Manager

Joanne's manager didn't waste time getting to the point. She simply asked her to talk about her workload and that of her employees. The contrast made the problem obvious. When Joanne explained her rationale, her manager would not buy it. She suggested that Joanne take a good look at her employees and their past work record. Most were high achievers when given the chance. She suggested that Joanne was afraid to let go of responsibility and authority and perhaps enjoyed *doing* work more than *managing* work. Joanne then admitted that perhaps she didn't know how to let go and still maintain control. The discussion concluded with Joanne's agreeing to attend a seminar on delegating and to work closely with her supervisor when she was unsure of how to proceed.

Case Study: The Hands-Off Supervisor

There are several things you could start doing to change this situation for the better:

- Assess the skills, experience, and training level of the new employees
- Talk with each of them about the types of work they would like delegated to them
- Focus on the management process of planning, organizing, motivating, and controlling

Appendix to Part 2

Comments & Suggested Responses

Case Study: Letting False Obstacles Get in the Way

1. Jerry used four false obstacles as excuses. He said that:
   - His people are inexperienced
   - He can't trust them
   - We can't afford mistakes
   - I don't have time to train
2. All the statements are true. Jerry may be working hard but as a manager, he is working at the wrong things. Jerry is probably very comfortable functioning as a task-oriented manager. But he needs to make a major change and begin focusing on the management process: planning, organizing, motivating, and controlling.

Appendix to Part 3

Comments & Suggested Responses

Case Study: Sometimes Consistent Results Aren't Enough

1. Are you a fair leader? If you had to answer *no* because you have not started developing your employees, it is time to get started. Set up an action plan as a guideline. If necessary, start your delegation plan with just one employee, then move on to the next.
2. Here you can list the positive things you do that show you are a fair leader.
3. If you answered *no*, this is where you describe what you are going to do about starting to delegate. An action plan that spells out who, what, where, and when will get you started.
4. What did you delegate to Jenny? Did you provide a worthwhile and interesting assignment for her? Review what you wrote. If you were in Jenny's shoes, would you welcome this assignment?

   What did you delegate to Eames? (Answer same questions as above.)
5. Cynthia needs to start a delegation plan and start focusing more on the management process rather just results. All her team members should be included. Before sitting down again with her manager, Crawford, she would be smart to have a plan in place. She should also have a developmental program for Jenny and Eames. Results are important but development of people through delegating meaningful work is also essential. Quality managers get good results and develop their people.

Case Study: The Delegation Disaster

Gino is to be commended for realizing the need to delegate, but he moved too quickly without preparing the delegations properly.

Gino should have taken the time to get to know his people and learn about each one's needs, abilities, and goals. It would also have been helpful to share his management style and personal goals for the organization. A gradual increase in delegated tasks, including practice in decision-making, would have been less threatening to the employees, since they did not seem to understand delegation or have confidence in their ability to undertake new assignments.

Gino's example is a good one. Delegation cannot just be forced on employees. It should be carefully planned and carried out if it is going to be successful.

Exercise: Mix and Match

Work Assignments to be Delegated	**Delegated to**
A. Redesign the month-end employee report	Steve, Davis, Zack
B. Train the employees on the new procedures	Davis, Zack
C. Conduct new product research	Logan, Steve, Davis, Zack
D. Lead a discussion on improving the work process	Steve, Davis
E. Write a job description for HR to use	Logan, Davis, Zack
F. Help design training for new employees	Susan, Davis, Zack
G. Participate in annual review with upper management	Davis
H. Present a safety topic at the next staff meeting	Logan, Susan
I. Summarize monthly reports for the unit	Steve, Davis, Zack
J. Fill in as the acting supervisor	Davis

There are many combinations of employees who might take on these assignments. If your answers are close to the ones above, you are on the right track.

Case Study: Delegating for Individual Development

Rich has a good developmental plan going for Megan and Bill. But to improve it, he needs to discontinue delegating work that requires use of their strong skills and provide them with assignments that will help build their weaker skills. Bill needs to be assigned work that will develop his analytical skills while Megan needs development of her leadership potential. If Megan and Bill were promoted or assigned more responsible positions and these skills weren't developed, it would reflect poorly on everyone involved. It's normal and practical to delegate to one's strength. But once the employee has demonstrated mastery in a particular skill it's time to move on and delegate work that will develop other skills.

Appendix to Part 4

Comments & Suggested Responses

Case Study: The Parking Lot Case

What steps did Alex miss?

Step 2: Gathering facts, feelings, and opinions

Step 4: Identifying all possible solutions

Step 5: Evaluating alternatives

You may have noted others as well.

If you were Alex's manager, you would need to assess his skills before delegating this assignment to him. You would also need to pay attention to the level of authority you provide in the delegation. And you definitely want to know what he is going to do before he carries out a solution. Alex has a lot of initiative, and as his manager you would need to help him develop strong problem-solving skills.

Case Study: One Problem After Another

The problems Salma encountered are as follows:

1. Getting enough girls to sign up
2. Only one week to prepare her team to play
3. Needs a place to practice
4. Outside gym is too expensive
5. Has to hold evening practices
6. Two girls can't practice in the evenings
7. Needs uniforms
8. No transportation for away games
9. Needs basketballs
10. Best player can practice only one day a week
11. Parent complaint
12. Uniforms aren't ready in time
13. Uniform supplier demands payment

Each step of the way, Salma faced a problem. Often one problem led to another. As you delegate work, you may see something similar happening. In this case, if you were the one giving Salma this assignment, you would have wanted to know ahead of time how much she knew about facilities and planning, along with her knowledge of the game. You would need to clearly discuss resources and levels of authority. And you would need to offer specific types of support. Salma created a winning team in spite of the problems she faced; you could help her develop her planning and problem-solving skills as well.

Case Study: Poor Work by Competent Employees

If you answered true to each question you get an *A*. Marla thinks she is delegating but she does not seem to know how to let go. She clearly has problems with the approach she uses in handing off the claims assignments. She hands them all off in the same way, not considering the individuals. Each employee has a different set of abilities. As you delegate to your employees, keep this in mind. With some, you can just say, "Do it," while others need lots of help.

In the case study, Marla does not see herself as the problem. Her representatives are probably frustrated. They handle unusual claims but they cannot make any decisions, nor do they talk to outside sources. Their investigations are completely dependent on Marla's input. She has not considered different levels of authority in her delegation process. She also does not see following through as support; she keeps all follow-up actions for herself in a controlling manner.

Case Study: The Reluctant Employee

In this case study, Petra responded well to Saul's direction and delegation. What might you do if she had not? If Petra failed to satisfactorily complete the assigned work, she needs to be held accountable and should be required to present an explanation. Perhaps Petra needs to be reminded why the work was assigned to her in the first place. Petra needs to understand that the delegated work was for her benefit and growth.

As Petra's manager, you need to let her know how disappointing her performance was. Serious discussion with Petra regarding any future assignments should take place. Be sure that Petra understands why she failed and perhaps offer some training in decision making.

You may also need to talk about whether it is best to give her more assignments at this point. Is she interested in doing delegated work? If yes, what assurances can she offer that the work will be done correctly? Is she interested in improving her skills and abilities? Perhaps Petra lacks motivation at this point and isn't interested in enhancing her knowledge and skills.

Not every employee can be developed. All employees deserve a chance, but they must commit to the delegated work and concentrate on its success.

Appendix to Part 5

Comments & Suggested Responses

Case Study: Implementing Change

Terence is smart to get his employees involved in the change process. He might meet with the entire group and talk about how the objectives could be reached. From that meeting, groups could be formed to study how to meet the objective. His team would probably have ideas on how to cut the budget by 10%.

Certain team members are likely to step up and demonstrate more motivation than others. These people can be the leaders of any subgroups that are formed. Emphasis can be placed on conducting valid research as to the various components of the budget.

Terence's team should be receptive to being involved. Their ideas will have value. If the group can come up with a way to reduce the budget by 10%, they will be considered a big success. Once the decision of how to cut the budget has been made, the employees will be more receptive to any necessary changes because they were part of the decision-making process.

Appendix to Part 6

Comments & Suggested Responses

Review

1. **False**. Think of how many excellent delegators you know.
2. **True**. If you are not delegating, you are not managing.
3. **True**. Chances are very good you will find someone who enjoys tasks you don't enjoy. We usually don't do very well on what we dislike.
4. **True**. Employees must grow in their skills if anyone in the organization is to advance, and you cannot do all the work yourself.
5. **False**. Employees usually appreciate the chance to make some decisions on their own.
6. **False**. Make a list of the tasks you cannot delegate. You will be amazed how short it is (if you are honest).
7. **False**. Research reflects just the opposite.
8. **True**. If you do not learn to delegate, your upward progress will stop, or you will burn out.
9. **True**. If you do not delegate, creativity can die.
10. **True**. Accomplishing results in key areas is what your job is all about.
11. **False**. Thought and preparation ensure success.
12. **True**. All of us need a chance to show what we can do.
13. **False**. Every employee has a different set of skills. When managers delegate work, some employees need a virtual road map on how to proceed, while others are capable of running on their own.
14. **True**. This is the critical condition.
15. **True**. Too often, managers delegate full authority or no authority.
16. **True**. Too much interference from the manager spoils the results.
17. **True**. Employees who can solve problems can work with more complex delegated tasks.
18. **True**. You need to spend your time being a manager, not doing operational tasks.

Additional Reading

Burns, Robert. *Making Delegation Happen*. Australia: Allen & Unwin Pty., Limited, 2002.

Chapman, Elwood N. and Wil McKnight. *The New Supervisor.* Boston, MA: Thomson Learning/Course Technology, 2003.

Chapman, Elwood N. and Barb Wingfield. *Winning at Human Relations.* Boston, MA: Thomson Learning/Course Technology, 2003.

Conlow, Rick. *Excellence in Supervision.* Boston, MA: Thomson Learning/Course Technology, 2001.

Dell, Twlya. *Motivating at Work.* Boston, MA: Thomson Learning/Course Technology, 1993.

Genett, Donna M. *If You Want It Done Right, You Don't Have to Do It Yourself!* Sanger, CA: Quill Driver Books, 2003.

Hathaway, Patti. *Giving and Receiving Feedback.* Boston, MA: Thomson Learning/Course Technology, 1998.

Huppe, Frank F. *Successful Delegation.* Franklin Lakes, NJ: Career Press Inc., 1994.

Lloyd, Sam R. *Accountability.* Boston, MA: Thomson Learning/Course Technology, 2002.

Minor, Marianne. *Coaching and Counseling.* Boston, MA: Thomson Learning/Course Technology, 2002.

Scott, Cynthia D. and Dennis T. Jaffe. *Empowerment.* Boston, MA: Thomson Learning/Course Technology, 1991.

Shea, Gordon F. *Mentoring.* Boston, MA: Thomson Learning/Course Technology, 2002.

Tepper, Bruce B. *Effective Delegation Skills*. West Des Moines, IA: American Media Publishing, 1997.

Ward, Michael E. and Bettye MacPhail-Wilcox. *Delegation and Empowerment.* Larchmont, NY: Eye on Education, 1999.

NOTES

NOTES

NOTES

NOTES

NOTES